A Brief History
of
The Fourteen Infallibles

WOFIS
World Organization for Islamic Services
Tehran -Iran

English translation:
First edition 1404/1984
Second edition 1413/1992.
Third edition 1422/2001

E-mail: wofis@wofis.com
http: //www. wofis. com

Published by
World Organization for Islamic Services,
P. 0. Box 11365-1545,
Tehran - 15837,
ISLAMIC REPUBLIC OF IRAN.

In the Name of Allah,
The All-compassionate, The All-merciful

Praise belongs to Allah, the Lord of all being,
the All-compassionate; the All-merciful;
the Master of the Day of Judgement;
Thee only, we serve, and to Thee alone we pray
for succour;
Guide us in the straight path;
the path of those whom Thou hast blessed,
not of those against whom Thou art wrathful,
nor of those who are astray.

O' Allah! send your blessings to the head of
your messengers and the last of
your prophets,
Muhammad and his pure and cleansed progeny.
Also send your blessings to all your
prophets and envoys.

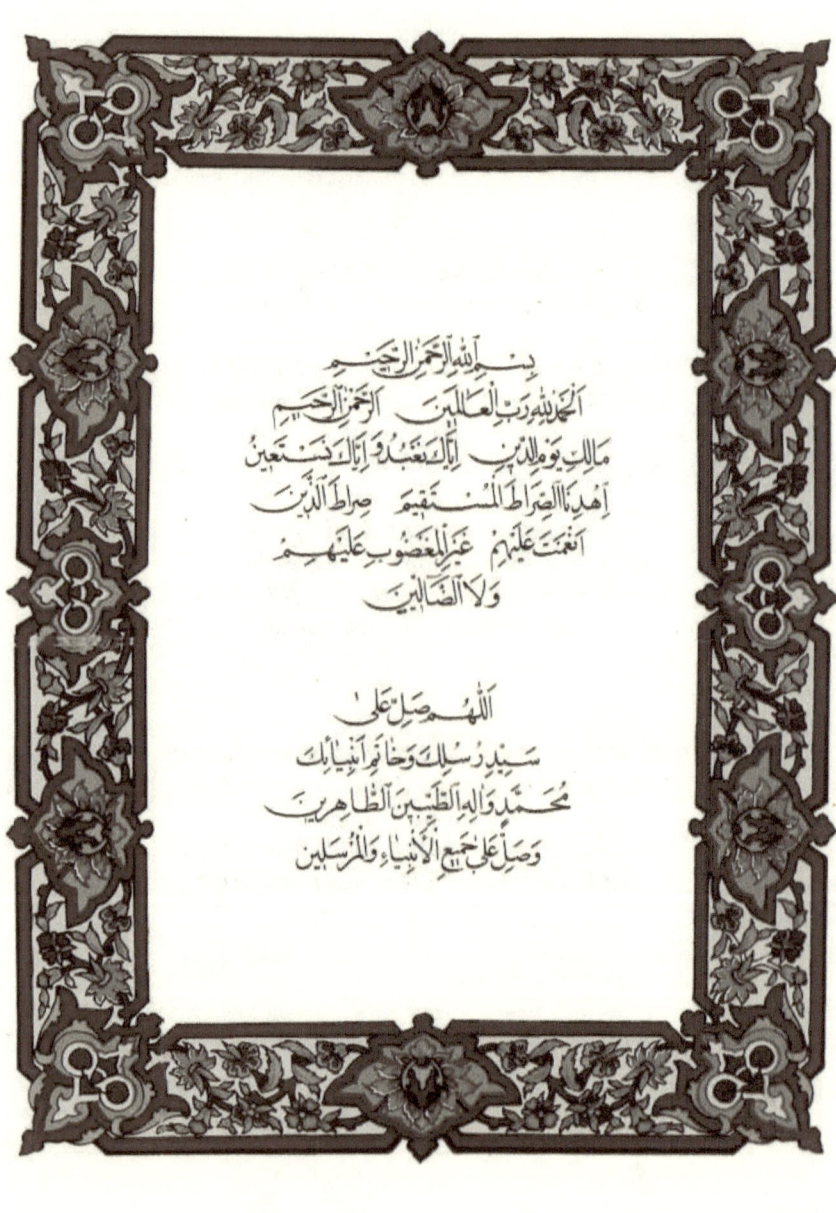

بِسْمِ اللهِ الرَّحْمَنِ الرَّحِيمِ

الْحَمْدُ لِلهِ رَبِّ الْعَالَمِينَ الرَّحْمَنِ الرَّحِيمِ

مَالِكِ يَوْمِ الدِّينِ إِيَّاكَ نَعْبُدُ وَإِيَّاكَ نَسْتَعِينُ

اهْدِنَا الصِّرَاطَ الْمُسْتَقِيمَ صِرَاطَ الَّذِينَ

أَنْعَمْتَ عَلَيْهِمْ غَيْرِ الْمَغْضُوبِ عَلَيْهِمْ

وَلَا الضَّالِّينَ

اللَّهُمَّ صَلِّ عَلَى

سَيِّدِ رُسُلِكَ وَخَاتَمِ أَنْبِيَائِكَ

مُحَمَّدٍ وَآلِهِ الطَّيِّبِينَ الطَّاهِرِينَ

وَصَلِّ عَلَى جَمِيعِ الْأَنْبِيَاءِ وَالْمُرْسَلِينَ

CONTENTS

CONTENTS

THE SECOND INFALLIBLE
THE DAUGHTER OF THE HOLY PROPHET

THE THIRD INFALLIBLE
THE FIRST IMkM

CONTENTS

CONTENTS

THE FIFTH INFALLIBLE
THE THIRD IMAM

THE SIXTH INFALLIBLE
THE FOURTH IMAM

THE SEVENTH INFALLIBLE
THE FIFTH IMAM

THE EIGHTH INFALLIBLE
THE SIXTH IMAM

CONTENTS

CONTENTS

TRANSLITERATION

Symbol	Transliteration	Symbol	Transliteration
ء		ل	I
ب	b	م	m
ت ث	t	ن	n
ث	th	و	w
ج	J	ه	h
ح	h	ي	Y
خ	kh	ة	ah
د	d		*Long Vowels*
ذ	dh	ا	a
ر	r	و	u
ز	z	ى	i
س	s		
ش	sh		*Short Vowels*
ص	s	´	a
ض	d	ُ	u
ط	t	ِ	i
ظ	z		
ع			*Persian Letters*
غ	gh	پ	P
ف	f	چ	ch
ق	q	ژ	zh
ك	k	گ	g

xv

تَصْدِير

لهذا الكتاب (التاريخ الموجز لأربعة عشر معصوما) تاريخ موجز ايجاز الكتاب نفسه. انّ أحد اخواننا الذى يعيش في بيئة تتكلّم بالانجليزية كان يؤلمه أن يرى الكثير من أبناء الشّيعة الّذين نشئوا وعاشوا في تلك البيئة أو في بيئات تشبهها لايكادون يفقهون إلّا لغة الوسط الّذى يعيشون فيه، و أنّ صلتهم باللّغة العربيّة أو غيرها من اللّغات الإسلاميّة قد انقطعت أوكادت، وبهذا قد انقطعت عنهم المادّة الّتي كان بإمكانها أن تمدّهم بمعرفة دينهم و أحكامهم، و أئمّتهم، و تاريخهم.

و لما كان عليه أخونا العزيز هذا من الغيرة للإسلام ومسائله والمسلمين و مشاكلهم، و من الإخلاص في العمل والسّعي بكلّ ما أوتي من حول و طول، عمد إلى تأليف كتاب حول سيرة المعصومين الأربعة عشر، سلام الله عليهم أجمعين قد انتزعه من ثلاثة مصادر: (الشّيعة في الإسلام) للمغفور له العلّامة الطباطبائيّ، وكتيّب في الموضوع نفسه للاستاذ شاكر، وكتب الاستاذ يوسف لالجي، فانتزع من هذه المصادر الثّلاثة فصولا لاءم بينها، و عمد إلى مواضع فأضاف وحذف، وكلّ ذلك لكي يلائم بين فصول الكتاب وحاجة المستوى العام لأبناء الشّيعة المغتربين، ولكي يسدّ عوز من لا يسمح لهم مستواهم الثّقافيّ بالرّجوع إلى المصادر الامّ، ويحول جهلهم باللّغات الإسلاميّة بينهم و بين الرّجوع إلى ما ألّف في تلك اللّغات ممّا يلائم مستواهم ويقضي حاجاتهم.

تَصْدِير

و قد أحال حفظه الله صنيعهُ هذا إلينا، فرأينا في الكتاب ما رآه هو، و آمنّا بما له من الفائدة المرجوّة بمثل ما آمن، فعقدنا العزم على نشر الكتاب، و نحن أيضا قد نظرنا في فصول الكتاب، فأخذنا في كثير من المواضع بما اقترحه، و أضفنا كثيرا من الملاحظات و أجرينا كثيرا من التّعديلات، كلّ ذلك تمشياً مع ما قدّمناه من الهدف الذي وضع الكتاب لبلوغه.

و من الله نسأل، أن يجعل فيه كلّ خير و بركة، و أن يثيب برحمته الّذين اشتركوا في اعداد هذا الكتاب، سواء الّذين كتبوا فصوله أوّل مرة، أو الّذين ألّفوا بينها، أو الّذين تناولوها بالإكمال وسعوا في ذلك إلى أن نجز العمل وتمّ الطبع والنّشر، و إليه عزّوجلّ نبتهل أن يسدّد خطانا، إنّه نعم المولى و نعم النصير.

المؤسّسة العالميّة للخدمات الإسلاميّة   ١٤٠٤/١٠/١

(لجنة التّأليف والتّرجمة والنّشر)   ١٩٨٤/٧/١

طهران — ايران

PREFACE

The Book: A *Brief History of the Fourteen Infallibles* has a concise history also. In brief, one of our brothers who is living in an English speaking country used to suffer from the isolation of his fellow Shi`ites and their poor knowledge of their history, their Imams, their school of thought and other related religious matters. This is due to the lack of information available in the English language and their own deficiencies in Arabic or other Islamic languages which could provide them with the necessary background and references.

This dear brother of ours was so dedicated to Islam and keen on finding a solution to help his Muslim brothers that he thought of compiling a concise book about the history of the Fourteen Infallibles, (i. e. the Prophet, his daughter az-Zahra' and the Twelve Imams, peace be on them). For his research he depended on three main works: the first, *Shi'ite Islam* by the late al-Allamah at-Tabataba'i, and, another booklet of Mr. Shakir and some works of Mr. Yousuf N. Lalljee. The author very ably found the necessary materials. He then made appropriate selections from them and classified these writings to meet the immediate need of those Shi'ahs who do not have access to these original sources.

He, may Allah protect him, gave us his work for critique. We found it interesting and relevant to aims that he and we are pursuing. We decided to publish the book after looking at his suggestions, and the sections of the book, adding some notes, deleting some sections, reshaping and editing to make it as perfect as possible.

Lastly, we pray to Allah to bless this work and those who shared in making contributions of all kinds by all means and methods: writing the original texts, selecting suitable sections, editing the work, and publishing the book.

We pray to Allah to guide our steps and to lead us in the right path, for He is the Best Master and the Best Helper.

WORLD ORGANIZATION FOR ISLAMIC SERVICES
(Board of Writing, Translation and Publication)

1/10/1404
1/ 7/1984
Tehran - IRAN.

THE SPIRITUAL MESSAGE OF SHI'ISM

The message of Shi'ism to the world can be summarized in one sentence: "To know God." Or in other words, it is to instruct man to follow the path of Divine realization and the knowledge of God in order to gain felicity and salvation. And this message is contained in the very phrase with which the Holy Prophet commenced his prophetic mission when he said: "Oh men! Know God in His Oneness (and acknowledge Him) so that you will gain salvation."

As a summary explanation of this message we will add that man is attached by nature to many goals in this worldly life and to material pleasures. He loves tasty food and drink, fashionable dress, attractive palaces and surroundings, a beautiful and pleasing wife, sincere friends and great wealth. And in another direction he is attracted to political power, position, reputation, the extension of his rule and dominion and the destruction of anything that is opposed to his wishes. But in his inner and primordial God-given nature, man understands that all these are means created for man, but man is not created for all these things. These things should be subservient to man and follow him and not vice versa. To consider the stomach

and the region below it as a final end of life is the logic
of cattle and sheep. To' tear up, cut and destroy others
is the logic of the tiger, the wolf and the fox. The logic
inherent in human existence is the attainment of wisdom
and nothing else.

This logic based upon wisdom with the power which
it possesses to discern between reality and the unreal,
guides us toward the truth and not toward things our
emotions demand or toward passions, selfishness and
egoism. This logic considers man as a part of the totality
of creation without any separate independence or the
possibility of a rebellious self-centeredness. In contrast
to the current belief that man is the master of creation
and tames rebellious nature and conquers it to force it
to obey his wishes and desires, we find that in reality
man himself is an instrument in the hand of Universal
Nature and is ruled and commanded by it.

This logic based upon wisdom invites man to con-
centrate more closely upon the apprehension he has of
the existence of this world until it becomes clear to him
that the world of existence and all that is in it does not
issue from itself but rather from an Infinite Source. He
will then know that all this beauty and ugliness, all these
creatures of the earth and the heavens, which appear out-
wardly as independent realities, gain reality only through
another Reality and are manifested only in Its Light, not
by themselves and through themselves. In the same way
that the "realities" as well as the power and grandeur of
yesterday have no greater value than tales and legends
of today, so are the "realities" of today no more than
vaguely remembered dreams in relation to what will appear as "reality" tomorrow. In the last analysis, everything in il'self is no more than a tale and a dream. Only
God is Reality in the absolute sense, the One Who does

not perish. Under the protection of His Being, everything gains existence and becomes manifested through the Light of His Essence.

If man becomes endowed with such vision and power of apprehension, then the tent of his separative existence will fall down before his eyes like a bubble on the surface of water. He will see with his eyes that the world and all that is in it depend upon an Infinite Being who possesses life, power, knowledge and every perfection to an infinite degree. Man and every other being in the world are like so many windows which display according to their capacity the world of eternity which transcends them and lies beyond them.

It is at this moment that man takes from himself and all creatures the quality of independence and primacy and returns these qualities to their Owner. He detaches himself from all things to attach himself solely to the One God. Before His Majesty and Grandeur he does nothing but bow in humility. Only then does he become guided and directed by God so that whatever he knows he knows in God. Through Divine guidance he becomes adorned with moral and spiritual virtue and pure actions which are the same as Islam itself, the submission to God, the religion that is in the primordial nature of things.

This is the highest degree of human perfection and the rank of the perfect man (the Universal Man; *insan-e kamel),* namely the impeccable Imam who has reached this rank through Divine grace. Furthermore, those who have reached this rank through the practice of spiritual methods, with the different ranks and stations that they possess, are the true followers of the Imam. It becomes thus clear that the knowledge of God and of the Imam are inseparable in the same way that the knowledge of God is inextricably connected to the knowledge of oneself.

For he who knows his own symbolic existence has already come to know the true existence which belongs solely to God who is independent and without need of anything whatsoever. (at-Tabataba'i, S. M. H., Shi`ite Islam, London, 1975, pp.215-217.)

THE GLORIOUS QUR'AN

The Glorious Qur'an (*Qur'anu 'l-Majid*) is the Word of Allah as revealed to His Prophet, Muhammad, peace be on him and his progeny.

From the time of its revelation till today, people have tried to cast doubt about the Divinity of the Holy Qur'an, but they have not succeeded because of its inherent truth. The Book itself gives guidance and wisdom, and it has a lot of good to offer to humanity. Every right minded reader, can derive a lot of benefit from it.

The Book of Allah constantly appeals to one to think, ponder and understand; and forbids one to drown one's reason or believe blindly. About six-hundred million Muslims believe in it, live and die by it.

To every prophet, Allah gave some miracle, but gone are the prophets and their miracles. The Holy Prophet Muhammad, peace be on him and his progeny, is the Last Prophet of Allah Who gave him an unperishable miracle and that miracle is the Holy Qur'an.

The Word of Allah (Kalamu 'llah, i.e., the Holy Qur'an) is a wonderful piece of poetry and Arabic literature, full of wisdom and guidance. On reading it one is at once convinced that it is the Word of Allah, for no man can write such perfect guidance on so many subjects.

The Holy Qur'an says that no man will be able to forge even a part of it and that no corruption shall touch it from any side. It is a miracle that the Holy Qur'an has remained unchanged and unaltered during all these 1400 years and it shall remain so till the Day of Resurrection, for Allah, has taken it on Himself to protect it.

The Book of Allah is like an ocean. The less learned, like children, collect pebbles and shells from its shores. The scholars and thinkers, like pearl divers, bring out from it the highest philosophy, wisdom and rules of a perfect way of living.

In order to understand the Glorious Qur'an, it is necessary to know the lives of Muhammad, `Ali, Fatimah, Hasan and Husayn, who translated every command and order of Allah into action. Muhammad being the perfect example for men, Ali for youths, Fatimah for women and Hasan and Husayn for children.

It is not necessary to refer to, or quote scholars, translators, commentators and narrators to prove the existence of Allah and His Prophet Muhammad.

Allah is the Creator, and He exists whether one believes it or not. The proof of His existence is His creation. The proof of Muhammad's prophethood is the Holy Qur'an.

For those who want to believe, these proofs are enough, and those who do not want to believe, will never believe, no matter what proofs or arguments, however strong they may be, are brought before them.

For easy daily recitation, the Qur'an is divided into thirty equal parts. One part takes only twenty-four reading minutes, and the whole Book requires twelve reading hours. There are 114 chapters, and 6,226 verses, containing 99,464 words made up of 330,113 letters.

Millions of Muslims read the Qur'an daily. Imam Ja'far as-Sadiq has said that, the minimum daily reading of the

Qur'an should be fifty verses or one-fourth of the part, about five minutes reading.

Historical and scholarly footnotes have been specially avoided to keep the volume from becoming cumbersome. Those interested in deeper studies, should have recourse to several libraries. (Shakir, M. A. ; Islamic History)

*   *   *   *   *

ISLAM AND MUSLIM

The word `islam'` means, submission to the will of Allah, and a `muslim',` `is` he who submits to the will of Allah.

Islam is a religion, which can be followed easily by everyone, everywhere, in a day to day life.

It is the religion of every prophet of Allah from Adam to Muhammad, and is as old as humanity. In fact, every child that is born, is a Muslim. It is the parents that make him a Jew, Christian or Hindu, etc.

Allah has sent numerous prophets to all the nations and races. As the human race progressed, the prophets were sent with laws that suited the requirements of that time. Each new prophet, brought a new Divine Law (*shari`ah*), which abrogated or cancelled the previous law.

Muhammad is the Last Prophet of Allah and he has brought the last and the most perfect law, in the Holy Qur'an. History shows us, that this law has suited the requirements of the people for the last 1400 years and shall continue to do so, till the Day of Resurrection.

Islam is a way of life. It is a simple and uncomplicated religion, giving one maximum freedom without encroaching on the freedom of others. It enjoins one to believe in One God, and do good; to keep up prayers and pay the poor-rate; to fast during the month of *Ramadan;*

xxxi

to perform the *hajj* and to fight for the sake of Allah, whenever necessary; to believe in the Justice of Allah, in the life after death, in the Prophethood of Muhammad and the teachings of the twelve Apostolic Imams. Islam forbids evil and tyranny, prohibits intoxicants and games of chance, adultery and indecencies, and blood and flesh of swine and dead animals.

There is no compulsion in religion (2:256) ; and there is no harsh and hard rituals or unreasonable dogmas in Islam.

Among many reforms, which the Holy Prophet of Islam, gave to the world, he taught, that all human beings whether brown, black, red, white or yellow, are sons of Adam, and no man has any superiority over another man, because of his colour, rank or riches. He taught:

The most honourable man, in the sight of Allah, is he, who is most careful of his duty to Allah and that man has rights only to the extent of the duties, he performs.

(Shakir, M.A.: *Islamic History)*

THE FIRST INFALLIBLE

THE HOLY PROPHET
OF
ISLAM

MUHAMMAD IBN ` ABDULLAH
(Peace be on him and his progeny)

Name: **Muhammad**
Title: al-Mustafa.
Agnomen: Abu '1-Qasim.
Father's name: Abdullah ibn Abdi '1-Muttalib.
Mother's name: Aminah bint Wahb.
Birth: Born in Mecca on Friday, 17th *Rabi `u '1-awwal*, in the Year of Elephant.
Death: Died at the age of 63 in Medina on Monday, 28th Safar, 11 AH; buried in his apartment adjoining the mosque, in Medina.

Lineal Chart of the Prophets

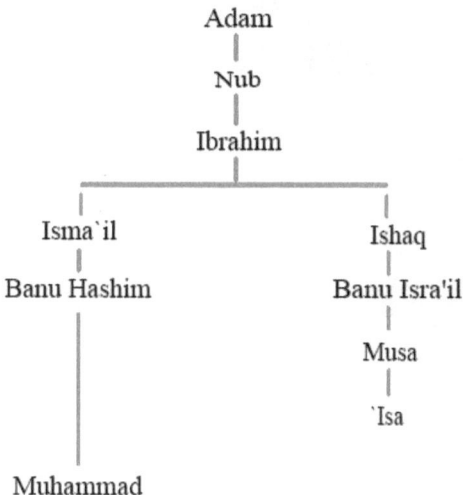

3

THE HOLY KA'BAH, MECCA.

LINEAGE

The Holy Prophet said:

The first thing God created was my nur (light).

The oldest and noblest tribe in the whole of Arabia was Ban& Hashim. They were the descendants of Ibrahim through his son Isma'il. The Arabs respected and loved them for their goodness, knowledge and bravery.

'ABDU 'L-MUTTALIB

'Abdu '1-Muttalib was the chieftain of Banu Hashim and lie was also the guardian of the Ka'bah.

Among his ten sons, 'Abdullah was the father of the Holy Prophet and Abu Talib was the father of 'Ali.

MUHAMMAD

In Mecca, baby boy Muhammad was born on 17th *Rabi 'u 'l-awwal,* 570 AD. His father 'Abdullah, son of 'Abdul '1-Muttalib, died before he was born and when he was six, he lost his loving mother Aminah bint Wahb.

5

His grandfather, `Abdu '1-Muttalib, took the responsibility of bringing up the orphan. At the age of ten, he was berefted of his venerable grandfather. On his death bed, he appointed his son Abu Talib as the guardian of Muhammad.

Gentle, soft spoken, tall and handsome boy, Muhammad, accompanied the trading caravans of Abu Talib, across the deserts, giving him deep insight into nature and man.

In his youth, Muhammad participated in Hilf (Confederation of) al-Fudul for helping the widows and orphans and protecting the oppressed.

KHADIJAH

The wealthy noble widowed lady Khadijah, looking for a manager for her rich mercantile caravans, selects Muhammad, the Trustee. Able and fair dealing, Muhammad is a tremendous success. Khadijah already an admirer, made him an offer of marriage, Muhammad was twenty-five and Khadijah forty. In spite of this disparity in age, the marriage proved to be a very happy one.

THE PROPHET

Lover of nature and quite, worried about human sufferings, Muhammad very often retired to Mount Hira' for meditations. One night, *laylatu 'l-qadr* (the Night of Majesty) a voice addressing him, commanded *"Recite in the Name of thy Lord."* Deeply excited by the strange phenomena of Divine Visitation, Muhammad hurried home to his wife, Khadijah, who listened to him attentively and said that "I bear witness that you are the Apostle of God."

After an interval, the voice from heaven spoke again *"O thou shrouded in thy mantle, arise, and warn, and magnify thy Lord. "* This was a signal for him to start preaching the gospel of truth of One God. In the beginning Muhammad invited only those near him, to accept the new Faith. The first to embrace Islam among women was Khadijah and among men `Ali. Soon after, Zayd ibn al-Harithah became a convert to the new Faith followed by Abu Bakr and `Uthman. `Umar hitheto a violent opponent of Islam, notorious for the persecution of the Muslims and a bitter enemy of the Prophet, embraced Islam, later.

CALIPH

For three long years, he laboured quietly to wean his people from the worship of idols and drew only thirty followers. Muhammad now decided to appeal publicly to the Quraysh to give up idol worship and embrace Islam.

He invited forty of his kinsmen to a feast. At the gathering, Muhammad stated that he had lived a lifetime among them and asked if they had ever found him lying? The general response was "We have never found you lying, O al-Amin! " The Prophet of Islam asked if he were to tell them that their enemies had collected beyond the sarid-hills to attack them, would they believe? The reply was, "Yes." "Will you believe anything I will now say?" Again the reply was, "Yes." The Prophet addressed them:

I know no man in all Arabia, who can offer his kindreds, a more excellent thing than I now do. I offer you happiness both in this life and that which is to come. God Almighty has commanded me to call unto Him. Who, therefore, among you will assist me herein shall become my Brother and my Caliph?

All of them hesitatingly declined the matter. `Ali ( who was then given the title of "Amiru '1-Mu'minin" - the Commander of the faithful - by the Prophet) stood up and declared that he would assist the Prophet and vehemently threatened those who would oppose him. Muhammad with great demonstration of affection, em- braced `Ali and declared to all, to hear and obey `Ali as his Deputy and Caliph. The gathering broke out into laughter, taunting Abu Talib that now he will have to obey his son.

ISLAM

Muhammad is the founder of the great religion of Islam, meaning submitting (oneself or one's person to Allah). The adherent of Islam is usually designated by the corresponding adjective Muslim. The Persians adopted a different adjective *Musalman,* from which are derived the Anglo-Indian *Mussulman.* But Muslims, certainly, dis- like the terms Mohammedan and Mohammedanism, which seem to them to carry the implication of worship of Muhammad, as Christian and Christianity imply the wor- ship of Christ.

The new Faith, is simple without complications, practical and useful for every day life. It commands to believe and do good, keep up prayer and pay the poor rate. Two orders giving four principles of a successful way of life.

The new Creed had set in motion a terrific revolution, shaking the very foundations of the world. The vested interests, kings, priests, racketeers, and tyrants all were

against, and they united to crush the movement of Islam.
The keepers of Ka'bah and owners of the idols, came to Abu Talib to stop Muhammad from saying, "There is no god but ALLAH (*la ilaha illa Allah*)." The guardian uncle conveyed the request of the delegation to give Muhammad fortune larger than possessed by any, to make him a chief and even a king, if he agreed to give up his mission. Muhammad refused. Angry Arab chieftains threatened social boycott, destruction and death. Abu Talib (who actually became Muslim but did not announce his faith so that he may be able to defend the Prophet) promised to defend Muhammad.

Boys and louts of Mecca started pelting stones and abuses on Muhammad. Brave and loyal `Ali, son of Abu Talib, stopped this by his strong fists. The harrassment and tortures, which the Prophet and his small band of faithful followers suffered at the hands of Quraysh were excruciating in the extreme. Some of the believers were dragged   over burning sand, imprisoned, flogged and starved, but they firmly held to their Faith till death. Umayyah, master of Bilal, took Bilal to the desert and exposed him bare-back with his face, to the noon-day sun and placed a big stone on his chest and said, "There you shall remain, until thou art dead or thou hast adjured Islam." Dying with thirst in the heat he would only answer *"A hadun! A hadun!* (One [God] ! One!)."

Almost ten years of hard work and preaching, in spite of all persecution, produced over a hundred followers. Physical cruelties and social boycott made life unbearable in Mecca. The Holy Prophet of Islam advised his followers, to seek refuge in the neighbouring country of Eithopia. Eighty-eight men and eighteen women sailed to the hospitable shores of the Negus, under the leadership of Ja'far at-Tayyar (brother of `Ali) and the cousin of the Holy Prophet. Arab chieftains pursued them and demanded their extradition.

Ja'far pleading the cause of the refugees said to the king

O King! we were plunged in the depth of ignorance and barbarism; we worshipped idols, we lived in unchastity, we ate dead bodies and we spoke abominations; we disregarded every feeling of humanity and the duties of hospitality and neighbourhood; we knew no law, but of the strong (power), when God raised among us a man, of whose birth, truthfulness, honesty and purity we are aware; and he called us to the Unity of God and taught us not to associate anything with Him; he forbade us the worship of idols; and enjoined on us to speak the truth, to be faithful to our trusts, to be merciful and to regard the rights of neighbours; he forbade us to speak evil of women or to eat the sustenance of orphans; he ordered us to fly from vice and to abstain from evil; to offer prayers, to render alms, to observe the fast. We have believed in him, we have accepted his teachings and his injunction to worship God and not associate anything with Him. For this reason our people have risen against us, have persecuted us in order to make us forego the worship of God and return to the worship of idols of stone and wood and other abominations. They tortured and injured us, until finding no safety among them, we have come to thy country and hope wilt protect us from their oppression.

The demand of the Quraysh were rejected and they returned to Mecca.

Several times the chieftains came to Abu Talib saying, "We respect your age and rank, but we have no further patience with your nephew. Stop him or we shall fight you."

Abu Talib asked Muhammad for his decision. With tears in his eyes the Apostle firmly replied, "O my uncle! if they place the sun on my right hand and the moon on my left, to force me to renounce my mission, I will not desist until God manifests His cause or I perish in the attempt."

TRAGEDIES

In a period of troubles, trials and tribulations two major tragedies afflicted Muhammad. First the venerable guardian uncle Abu Talib died and shortly afterwards his noble wife Khadijah died, leaving behind her daughter Fatimah (peace be on her) - the only child she had from the Holy Prophet - the daughter who looked after her father so much so that the Prophet called her *Umm abiha* (the mother of her father).

MUSLIM ERA

With the death of the old patriarch Abu Talib, the Meccans planned to assassinate the Prophet. Under Divine guidance, he asked 'Ali to sleep in his bed and Muhammad put his green garment on 'Ali. While the murderers mistook Ali for Muhammad, the Holy Prophet of Islam escaped to Medina. (See photo on p.12)

The Muslim era of Hijrah (Emigration) is named after this incident and dated from 17th *Rabi 'u 'l-awwal,* 622 AD.

From the time he came to Medina, he was the grandest figure upon whom the light of history has ever shone. We shall now see him as, the king of men, the ruler of

EXTERIOR VIEW OF THE PROPHET'S MOSQUE, MEDINA.

human hearts, chief law-giver and supreme judge. The Preacher who went without bread, was mightier than the mightiest sovereigns of the earth. No emperor with his tiaras was obeyed, as this man in a cloak of his own clothing.

He laid the foundation of the Muslim commonwealth and drew up a charter which has been acknowledged as the work of highest statemanship, a master-mind not only of his age, but of all ages.

Unlike the Arabs, the Prophet, had never wielded a weapon, but now he was forced to defend Islam by force of arms. Commencing from the battle of Badr, a series of eighty battles had to be fought, which the infant community defended successfully.

One day Muhammad was sleeping under a tree, away from his camp. He was awakened by his enemy Du'thur ibn al-Harith with sword, standing over him. "O Muham mad! Who is there now to save you? " "God! " replied the Apostle. The wild Bedouin suddenly began to shiver and dropped his sword. The Prophet picked the sword and asked, "Who is there now to save you?" "Alas, no one!" "Then learn from me to be merciful." The Arab's heart was overcome and he embraced Islam.

UHUD

Nex year, **Abu Sufyan** the famous long-lived **enemy** of Islam, again attacked the Muslims at Uhud. Hamzah, the first flag-bearer of Islam and uncle of the Prophet, was killed in action. In spite of strict instructions from the Prophet, a few Muslim soldiers deserted their post when victory was in sight. This changed the course of the battle. Khalid ibn al-Walid attacked the Prophet and

the grave situation was saved by the timely arrival of `Ali.
The enemies ran away and the issue was decided. Muhammad was deeply grieved at the death of Hamzah.

MUBAHILAH

In the 10th year AH a Christian deputation from
Najran came to the Prophet at Medina for religious discussions. Even after convincing arguments the Christians
refused to believe, because they were not willing to give
up their religion for the religion of Islam.

According to Divine instructions in the Holy Qur'an:

فَمَنْ حَآجَّكَ فِيهِ مِنْ بَعْدِ مَا جَآءَكَ مِنَ الْعِلْمِ فَقُلْ تَعَالَوْا نَدْعُ أَبْنَاءَنَا وَ أَبْنَاءَكُمْ وَ نِسَآءَنَا وَ
نِسَآءَكُمْ وَ أَنْفُسَنَا وَ أَنْفُسَكُمْ ثُمَّ نَبْتَهِلْ فَنَجْعَلْ لَعْنَتَ اللَّهِ عَلَى الْكَاذِبِينَ. (آل عمران، ٣/ ٦١)

*And whoso disputes with thee concerning him, after
the knowledge that has come to thee, say: "Come
now, let us call our sons and your sons, our women
and your women, our selves and your selves, then
let us humbly pray and so lay Allah's curse upon
the ones who lie." (3:61)*

Muhammad suggested that next morning, the Christians
should bring their women, sons and near ones and the
Prophet would bring his, and they should pray, to in-
voke the curse of God on the liars, in order to end the
argument.

At dawn Muhammad entered the *maydan* (field) with
his grandsons, leading Hasan by the hand, carrying Husayn
in his arms, his beloved daughter Fatimah following him
and Ali walking behind her, with the banner of Islam. The
Christians watching this procession from far, came to the
conclusion that Muhammad was the true Prophet of God,

for he had brought with him his dearest and nearest ones.

The Christians came to the Prophet and informed him that they were not willing to pray for the curse on the liars, instead they were willing to pay the *jizyah** and to come to a settlement. The Prophet referred them to Ali for terms.

HUDAYBIYYAH

The Muslims had been in self exile for six years and began to feel a keen yearning for their homeland, Mecca. The Prophet desired to perform a pilgrimage to Ka'bah. When he forsook his home town he was weak, but when he wanted to return, he was strong. He did not use his strength to force an entry into the sacred city. Finding the Quraysh hostile, Muhammad entered into a treaty known as the Peace of Hudaybiyyah, appearing not very advantageous to the Muslims, but which revealed the Islamic character of moderation and magnanimity. For the strong to excercise restraint and toleration is true courage. Having reached upto the door of their birth place with hearts over-flowing with impatient longing to enter it, the Muslims retraced their steps peacefully to Medina, under the terms of the treaty, which allowed them to perform the pilgrimage next year.

KHAYBAR

The harassment and murders by the Jews, forced the Prophet into leading an army against Khaybar in

---

*   Jizyah: poll-tax or tithes, payable by non-Muslims in the realm of Islam.

the 7th year AH. The Muslims under the command of
`Umar and others turned back and were in despair. The
Prophet said: "Tomorrow I shall assign the command
of the Muslim force to a person who will be crowned
by God with victory." The daybreak saw the Islamic
banner waving gallantly in the hand of `Ali. The fateful
battle began with Jewish champion warrior Marhab.
With soul stirring shout of *Allahu Akbar,* the Dhulfiqar
(sword) of `Ali descended on Marhab, piercing his skull.
In the general encounter that followed, the Jews were
defeated. The great victory of Islam was won and made
Ali the immortal conqueror of Khaybar.

MECCA

Towards the end of the year, Muhammad with his
followers availed of the truce of Hudaybiyyah to accomplish the pilgrimage to Mecca. For three days, the Quraysh
evacuated the city and watched the Muslims perform the
pilgrimage. The strict observance of the terms of treaty,
the self restraint and regard for their pledged word dis-
played by the believers, created a great impression on
the idolators. Struck by Muhammad's kindness of heart
and nobility of nature many Qurayshite chieftains adopted
the Faith.

In the 8th year AH, the idolators violated the peace
of Hudaybiyyah by attacking the Muslims. The enemies
were defeated and Mecca was conquered.

The Prophet who fled from Mecca as a fugitive, now
returned home as a mighty conqueror. The *Rahmatun lil
'alamin* (mercy unto all beings, i.e., the Prophet) entered
the city with his head bowed low in thankfulness to the
Almighty (Allah) and ordered a general amnesty, instead

of the mass massacre of those who persecuted him and
his followers.

TABUK

In the middle of the 9th year AH, the Prophet had to
lead an expedition to Tabuk near the border of Syria,
owing to the threatening attitude of the Roman Emperor.
The hypocrites and holders back out of spite, taunted `Ali,
who was left in charge of Medina in the absence of the
Prophet. Unable to bear the taunts of the hypocrites, the
brave and faithful `Ali mounted a fast camel and reached
the Muslim army. Ali related to the Prophet the taunts
of the hypocrites that `Ali was frightened and that the
Prophet was displeased with him. Muhammad smiled and
said: "O `Ali! do you not wish that your position with
me should be like Harun's position with Musa, with this
difference only, that after me there will be no prophet?"
The pacified Ali returned to Medina. The Muslim army
on reaching Tabuk found, the Romans had diverted to
other fields of action. The Prophet returned to Medina
without having to fight.

WIVES

A great number of Muslim soldiers were killed in
battles at Badr, Uhud, Khaybar, Hunayn and other places,
leaving behind young wives and children. The serious prob
lem of taking care of the widows and orphans, threatened
to break up the moral fabric of the Muslim Society.
Muhammad decided to marry these widows and set an
example for his followers to do likewise.

Before the advent of Islam, a man could marry any number of wives but the Holy Prophet of Islam was different in every way. History bears out, the unimpeach able character of Muhammad upto the age of twenty-five, when he married the widowed lady Khadijah. She remained his one and only wife till she died when Muhammad was fifty. At the ripe age of fifty-five when the blood cools down, in order to solve the problem of war, widows and orphans, he started marrying one wife after another in quick succession, even though he was old and burdened with the responsibilities of Prophethood and the affairs of the Islamic State.

The conditions for marrying more than one wife, are so strict, that hardly anybody can fulfil them, in times of peace. The Qur'an says:

وَإِنْ خِفْتُمْ اَلاَّ تُقْسِطُوا فِي الْيَتَامَى فَانْكِحُوا مَا طَابَ لَكُمْ مِنَ النِّسَآءِ مَثْنَى وَثُلثَ وَرُبَاعَ فَإِنْ
خِفْتُمْ اَلاَّ تَعْدِلُوا فَوَاحِدَةً . . .   (النِّسَاء، ٤/٣)

And if you fear that you cannot act equitably towards orphans then marry such women as seem good to you, two, three and four, but if you fear that you cannot do justice between them, then marry only one . . . (4:3)

KING

Though a Prophet and a King, Muhammad was the man of the common man. He sat and ate with them. Shared their joys and sorrows, helped the weak, widows and orphans and sympathized with the distressed. He found the world sunk deep in degrading ignorance, super-stition, vice and cruelty; he saw people disunited and engaged in perpetual wars, practising most revolting cruelties;

the daughters were buried alive and the widows of their fathers were inherited or sold by the eldest son. Among all this chaos, Muhammad established order and inspired in them the belief of One God; prohibited idolatory and made them think, not only of this world, but beyond the grave on a higher, purer and diviner plain, asking them to practise charity, goodness, justice, reasonableness and universal love. The whole mission was achieved in his lifetime.

THE FIVE PURIFIED ONES
(Ahlu 'l-Kisa')

إِنَّمَا يُرِيدُ اللهُ لِيُذْهِبَ عَنْكُمُ الرِّجْسَ أَهْلَ الْبَيْتِ وَ يُطَهِّرَكُمْ تَطْهِيرًا. (الاحزاب ، ٣٣/٣٣)

Allah only desires to keep away the uncleanliness from you, O People of the House! and purify you a (thorough) purifying. (Qur'an, 33:33)

The Five Purified Ones - **Muhammad**, **Ali**, **Fatimah**, and their two sons **Hasan** and **Husayn**- became perfect examples of human conduct. They lived a life of extreme devotion, loyalty, utility, goodness, trust and charity, giving a standard of human values to every action of humanity. Their record of life is that of a work nobly and faithfully done, preaching the Unity of God, the equality of men and obliterating the tyranny of priests and rulers, breaking the shackles of wrangling creeds, oppressive rituals, soul crushing dogmas; he broke down the barriers of caste, exclusive privileges and tyranny of vested interest. He proclaimed the importance of knowledge learning and hard work.

Though the Holy Prophet was occupied in looking after the affairs of people, but he used to pay special attention to his family too. Some believers, requested him to allow them to buy lands and build houses for him. The reply was revealed by God:

قُلْ لاَ أَسْئَلُكُمْ عَلَيْهِ أَجْراً إِلاَّ الْمَوَدَّةَ فِى الْقُرْبَى... إِنَّ اللّهَ غَفُورٌ شَكُورٌ. (الشُّورى، ٤٢/٢٣)

Say: "I do not ask of you any reward, but love for my relatives ... ; surely Allah is Forgiving, Grateful. "
(42:23)

Thereupon, the believers asked the Prophet whose love was made incumbent on them? Muhammad answered "Love for `Ali, Fatimah, Hasan and Husayn."

LAST PILGRIMAGE

Under the Divine intuition of his approaching end, Muhammad prepared to make the farewell pilgrimage to Mecca.

Before completing all the ceremonies of *hajj*, he addressed a huge multitude from the top of mount 'Arafat on 8th *Dhi 'l-hajjah,* 11 AH in words which shall ever ring and live in the atmosphere

O ye people! listen to my words, for I know not, if another year will be vouchsafed to me after this year, to find myself amongst you at this place. Your lives and property are sacred and inviolable to one another, until ye appear before the Lord, as this day and this month is sacred for all, and remember ye shall have to appear before your Lord, Who shall demand an account of all your actions. O ye people, ye have rights over your wives and your wives have rights over you. . . Treat your wives with kindness and love.

Verily, ye have taken them on the security of God and made their persons lawful unto you by the Words of God. Keep faithful to the trust reposed in you and avoid sins. Usury is forbidden. The debtor shall return only the principal and the beginning will be made with the loan of my uncle Abbas son of `Abdul-Muttalib. Henceforth the vengeance of blood practised in the days of ignorance is prohibited; and all blood feuds abolished, commencing with the murder of Ibn Rabi`ah son of al-Harith son of Abdul-Muttalib.

And your slaves! see that ye feed them with such food as ye eat yourselves, and clothe them with the stuff ye wear; and if they commit a fault which ye are not inclined to forgive, then part from them, for they are the servants of the Lord and are not to be harshly treated.

O ye people! listen to my words and understand the same, know all Muslims are brothers unto one another. Ye are one brotherhood, nothing which belongs to another is lawful unto his brother, unless freely given out of goodwill. Guard yourselves from committing injustice.

Let him that is present tell it unto him that is absent. Haply he that shall be told may remember better than he who hath heard it.

HADITH OF GHADIR

Soon after finishing the *hajj* the Holy Prophet started for Medina. On his way, at 'Ghadir Khumm' the Voice from Heaven cried:

يَآ أَيُّهَا الرَّسُولُ بَلِّغْ مَآ أُنزِلَ اِلَيْكَ مِنْ رَبِّكَ وَ اِنْ لَمْ تَفْعَلْ فَمَا بَلَّغْتَ رِسَالَتَهُ وَآللهُ يَعْصِمُكَ

مِنَ النَّاسِ اِنَّ اللهَ لاَ يَهْدِى الْقَوْمَ الْكَافِرِينَ .   (المائدة، ٥/٦٧)

O Apostle! deliver what has been revealed to you from your Lord; and if you do it not, then you have not *delivered His message and Allah will protect you from the people, surely Allah will not guide the unbelieving people** (5:67).

Muhammad immediately ordered Bilal to recall the Muslims, who had gone ahead, who were behind and who were proceeding to their homes at the junction, to assemble. The famous Sunni *mutakallim* and commentator, Fakhru 'd-Din ar-Razi in his *at-Tafsiru 'l-kabir,* (vol. 12, pp. 49 - 50), writes that the Prophet took `Ali by the hand and said:

مَنْ كُنْتُ مَوْلَاهُ فَعَلِيٌّ مَوْلَاهُ. اَللّٰهُمَّ وَالِ مَنْ وَالَاهُ وَ عَادِ مَنْ عَادَاهُ وَانْصُرْ مَنْ نَصَرَهُ وَاخْذُلْ مَنْ خَذَلَهُ.

Whoever whose *mawla* (master) I am, `Ali is his master. O Allah! love him who loves `Ali, and be the enemy of the enemy of `Ali; help him who helps `Ali, and forsake him who forsakes `Ali.

He (ar-Razi) writes further that Abu Bakr and `Umar congratulated `Ali in the following words:

هَنِيئاً لَكَ يَابْنَ أَبِي طَالِبِ أَصْبَحْتَ وَ اَمْسَيْتَ مَوْلَايَ وَ مَوْلَى كُلِّ مُؤْمِنٍ وَ مُؤْمِنَةٍ

Congratulations, O son of Abu Talib! This morning you became my *mawla* and *mawla* of every believing man and woman.

Once again the voice from Heaven proclaimed:

اَلْيَوْمَ اَكْمَلْتُ لَكُمْ دِينَكُمْ وَ اَتْمَمْتُ عَلَيْكُمْ نِعْمَتِي وَ رَضِيتُ لَكُمُ الْاِسْلَامَ دِيناً.
(الْمَائِدَة، ٥/٣)

This day have I perfected your religion and completed My favour on you and chosen for you Islam

---

* The *hadith* of Ghadir is *mutawatir* to Shi`ahs and Sunnis, because it has been narrated through so many chains of transmission by both sects that no doubt can be entertained. As, for the Shiite transmission of this *hadith* see *al-Bihar,* vol. 37, pp. 108 -253; and as for others see the book of *Imamate,* by S . S . A . Rizvi, part 2, pp. 39 - 105, 1985, WOF IS, Tehran - IRAN.

as a religion (5:3).

DEATH

On Muhammad's return to Medina, he got busy settling the organization of the provinces and the tribes which had adopted Islam. His strength rapidly failed and the poison (administered at Khaybar by a Jewess) took its deadly toll. So ended the life dedicated to the service of God and humanity from first to last, on 28th Safar, 11 AH.

The humble Preacher had risen to be the ruler of Arabia. The Prophet of Islam not only inspired reverence, but love owing to his humility, nobility, purity, austerity, refinement and devotion to duty. The Master inspired all who came into contact with him. He shared his scanty food; he began his meals in the Name of Allah and finished them uttering thanks; he loved the poor and respected them, he would visit the sick and comfort the heart broken; he treated his bitterest enemies with clemency and forbearance, but the offenders against society were administered justice; his intellectual mind was remarkably progressive and he said that man could not exist without constant efforts.

There is no god but One God and Muhammad is the Apostle of God, peace and blessings of Allah be upon him and his descendants.

The lives of Muhammad and ʿAli are so interwoven that one cannot think, read or write without mentioning both.

Imam Ali said:

"I testify that there is no god but Allah and I testify that Muhammad is the servant and Prophet of God sent with the famous Faith and the written Book with strong commands and prohibitions to remove the doubts and superstitions of the people and to give reasonings and proofs.

"He was sent to make the people fear the signs of God and His punishment. God has done us a big favour by giving us such a Prophet, so that we may follow him.

"Then Allah deputed Muhammad, peace be upon him and his progeny, as a witness, giver of good tidings and warner, the best in the universe as a child and the most chaste as a grown up man, the pcrest of the purified in conduct, the most generous of those who are approached for generosity.

"The hearts of the virtuous and good people turn to him. He has established brotherhood. His word is the Word of God. He gave them the Message of God without minimizing or magnifying it.

"He gives eyes to those who earnestly seek guidance and be recited the Holy Qur'an. He is the Fountain of Knowledge and Light of the World.

"He is a great Physician. The ointment of his knowledge is very effective and unfailing. He searches for houses where there is no peace and confusion reigns.

"May Allah give height to his (the Prophet's) construction above all other constructions, heighten his position with Thee, grant perfection to his effulgence and perfect for him his light. In reward for his discharging Thy prophetship, grant that his testimony be admitted and his speech be liked for his speech is just, and his judgments are clear-cut. May Allah put us and him together in the pleasures of life, continuance of bounty, satisfaction of desires, enjoyment of pleasures, ease of living, peace of mind and gifts of honour.

"He is Thy Trustee and knows Thy secrets. He shall

testify on the Day of Judgment. Reward him handsomely. Let him intercede for his followers, for he is just and can distinguish between right and wrong.

"All praise is due to Allah, who cannot even be imagined. No person, however, wise he may be, can understand Him.

"Muhammad is the last of all the prophets. There shall be no prophet after him. Revelation came to an end on his passing away. The sons of the Holy Prophet are the best sons and his *Ahlu 'l-bayt,* are the best *ahlu-l-bayt.* Follow your Apostolic Imams." (See photo p. 26)

SOME OF THE AHADITH OF
THE HOLY PROPHET

The Apostle of Allah was the handsomest of men and the most liberal and the most brave. He said:

1. Convey to others no words of mine save, those you know for a certainty.

2. Whosoever ascribes doctrines or precepts to me, and they are not mine, the same shall go to hell.

Backbiters:

3. A slanderer and backbiter shall be shut out from Paradise.

Charity:

4. Charity averts impending calamities.

5. The tax of Charity should be collected from the rich and given away to the poor.

6. A man giving in alms one piece of silver in his lifetime is better for him than giving one hundred when about to die.

INTERIOR VIEW OF THE COMPOUND OF THE
PROPHET'S MOSQUE, MEDINA.

7. To meet friends cheerfully and invite them to a feast are charitable acts.

8. To extend consideration towards neighbours and send them presents are charitable acts.

Death:

9. Wish not for death, before its time comes.

10. Speak well of your dead and refrain from speaking ill of them.

11. To commit suicide is one of the mortal crimes.

Dignity of Labour

12. Whoever is able and fit and does not work for himself or for others, Allah is displeased with him.

13. Those who can earn an honest living are the beloved of Allah.

14. Allah is Gracious to him who earns his living by his own labour and not by begging.

15. Whosoever opens unto himself the door of begging, Allah will open unto him the door of poverty.

16. O Allah! Keep me from inability and laziness.

17. Whoever monopolizes trade is a transgressor.

Education:

18. To acquire knowledge is binding upon all Muslims, whether male or female.

19. Man has free will and is responsible for his actions.

20. The ink of the scholar is more holy than the blood of the martyr.

21. He who travels in search of knowledge, to him Allah shows the way to Paradise.

22. Seek after knowledge though it be in China.

23. Acquire knowledge, because he who acquires it, in the way of the Lord, performs an act of piety; who

speaks of it praises the Lord; who seeks it, adores Allah; who dispenses instruction in it, bestows alms; and who imparts it to its fitting objects, performs an act of devotion to Allah. Knowledge enables its possessor to distinguish what is forbidden from what is not; lights the way to Heaven; it is our friend in the desert, our companion in solitude, our companion, when bereft of friends; it guides us to happiness; it sustains us in misery; it is our ornament in the company of friends; it serves as an armour against our enemies. With knowledge the creature of Allah rises to the heights of goodness and to noble position, associates with sovereigns in this world and attains the perfection of happiness in the next.

24. The worst of men is, a bad learned man and a good learned man is the best.

25. He dies not who takes to learning.

Enemies of Allah:

26. The greatest enemies of Allah are those who profess Islam and do acts of infidelity and who without cause, shed man's blood.

27. The Prophet said: "The mortal crimes are to associate another with Allah, to vex your father and mother, to murder your own species, to commit suicide and to swear to a lie."

Envy:

28. Do not look for the faults of others and do not envy others.

29. Keep yourselves far from envy, because it eats up and takes away good actions, like the fire that eats up and burns wood.

Fasting

30. A keeper of fast, who forsakes not lying and

slander, Allah cares naught for his leaving off eating and drinking.

Favoured of Allah:
31. Who is the most favoured of Allah? He from whom the greatest good comes to His creatures.

32. Verily Allah loves a Muslim who is poor with a family and withholds himself from what is unlawful and from begging.

Forgiveness
33. Whoever suppresses his anger, when he has in his power to show it, Allah will give him a great reward.

34. The person is most esteemed in the sight of Allah who pardons, when he has in his power, him who shall have injured him.

35. He is not strong and powerful, who throws people down, but he is strong who withholds himself from anger.

36. Thus said Allah: Verily, those who excercise patience under trials and forgive wrongs are righteous.

Hypocrites:
37. He is a hypocrite who when he speaks, speaks untruth; who making a promise breaks it; and who, when trust is reposed in him, fails in his trust.

38. Muslims are those who perform their trust, fail not in their word and keep their pledge.

Islam and Others:
39. One of the followers of the Prophet asked him to curse the infidels. The Prophet said: "I am not sent for this, nor was I sent but as a mercy to mankind."

40. Every child is born with a disposition towards the natural religion (Islam). It is the parents who make

it a Jew, a Christian or a Magian.

41. Deal gently with people, and be not harsh; cheer them and condemn not.

Manners:

42. Much silence and a good disposition; there are no two works better than these.

43. The best of friends is he who is best in behaviour and character.

44. The exercise of religious duties will not atone for the fault of an abusive tongue.

Marriage:

45. Marriage is incumbent on all who can afford or who possess the ability.

Modesty

46. One who does not practise modesty and does not refrain from shameless deeds is not a Muslim.

47. The adultery of the eye is to look with an eye of lust on the wife of another; and the adultery of the tongue is to utter what is forbidden.

48. 1 swear by Allah, there is not anything, which Allah so condemns, as his male and female servants committing adultery.

49. The person who drinks liquor, commits adultery and steals, calls upon himself severe punishment.

Muslims and Muslim Brotherhood:

50. A Muslim is he from whose tongue and hands Muslims are safe.

51. A true Muslim is thankful to Allah in prosperity and resigned to His will in adversity.

52. It is not worthy of a speaker of truth to curse

people.

53. That person is not a perfect Muslim who eats his full and leaves his neighbours hungry.

54. No man has believed perfectly, until he wishes for his brother that which he wishes for himself.

55. All Muslims are like one wall, some parts strengthening others; in such a way they must support each other.

56. Muslims are brothers in religion, and they must not oppress one another nor abandon assisting one another nor hold one another in contempt; and all things of one Muslim are unlawful to another, his blood, property and reputation.

57. To abuse a Muslim is disobedience to Allah and it is infidelity to fight with one.

58. The duties of Muslims to each other are six

    i. When you meet a Muslim *salam* (greet) him;

    ii. When he invites you to dinner, accept it;

    iii. When he asks you for advice give it to him;

    iv. When he sneezes and says *"al-Hamdu li 'llah"* (Praise be to Allah), you should say *"Rahimaka-'llah* (may Allah have mercy on you) ;

    v. When he is sick visit him; and

    vi. When he dies, follow his bier.

Oppression:

59. Allah loves not the tyrants and he desires not tyranny in the world.

Orphans:

60. The best Muslim house, is that in which an orphan is well cared for.

61. I and the guardian of orphans will be in one place in the next world like my two fingers, touching each other.

Qur'an, Prophet and His Near Relatives:

62. O Lord! grant to me the love of Thee; grant that I love those that love Thee; grant that I may do the deeds that win Thy love; make Thy love dearer to me than self, family or wealth.

63. Verily Allah instructs me to be humble and lowly and not proud, and that no one should oppress another.

64. The Prophet would go out in advance to receive his daughter Fatimah, when she came from her husband's house.

65. I have left two Precious Things among you and you will not go astray as long as you hold fast to them - one is the Book of Allah (Qur'an), and the other is my near relatives (Ahlu 'l-bayt).

66. I and `Ali are created from one *nur* (light).

67. I am the City of Knowledge and `Ali is its Gate.

68. O `Ali! your position with me is the same as Harun's was with Musa, with this difference only that there will be no prophet after me.

69. Whoever believes me to be his mawla, `Ali is also his mawla. O Lord! befriend him who befriends `Ali and be the enemy of the enemy of `Ali.

70. Fatimah is a piece of my heart.

71. Husayn is from me and I am from Husayn.

72. Hasan and Husayn are the leaders of youths of Paradise.

Paradise:

73. A person will not enter into Paradise, who has one atom of pride in his heart.

74. Hell is veiled in delights and Heaven in hardships and miseries.

75. They will enter the garden of Bliss who have a true, pure and merciful heart.

76. Guard yourselves from five things and I am your surety for Paradise:

    i. When you speak, speak the truth;

    ii. Perform when you promise;

    iii. Discharge your trust;

    iv. Withhold your hand from striking; and

    v. From taking that which is unlawful and bad.

Parents and Family:

77. Paradise lies at the feet of thy mother.

78. Allah's pleasure is in father's pleasure and Allah's displeasure is in father's displeasure.

79. He who wishes to enter Paradise must please his father and mother.

80. It is a pity, young persons may not attain Paradise by not serving their old parents.

81. A man must do good to his parents, although they may have injured him.

82. Kindness is a mark of faith and whoever has not kindness has no faith.

83. No father has given his children anything better than good manners.

84. Treat children with a view to inculcate self respect in them.

85. Whoever does good to daughters will be saved from Hell.

86. He is of the most perfect of Muslims, whose disposition is most liked by others.

Pride

87. No one who keeps his mind focussed entirely upon himself, can grow large, strong and beautiful in character.

88. A community must desist from boasting of their

ancestors. Mankind are all sons of Adam and he was from earth.

Reason:

89. The first thing created was my *nur* (light).

90. Honourable thoughts create honourable results.

Recommendations:

91. The greatest *jihad* is that for the conquest of self.

92. The best of acts in Allah's sight, is that which is constantly attended to, though it be in a small degree.

93. Trust in Allah but tie your camel.

94. The best of acts are found in the golden mean.

Remembrance of Allah:

95. A good disposition, deliberation in works and to adopt the golden mean in all affairs, are of the qualities of prophets.

96. There is a polish for everything and the polish for the heart is the remembrance of Allah.

97. Whoever loves to meet Allah, Allah loves to meet him.

98. The five stated prayers erase the sins which have been committed during the intervals between them, if they have not been mortal sins.

99. Say your prayers standing. If you are not able, do it sitting and if not sitting, do it in bed.

100. Order your children to say the stated prayers, when they are seven years of age and punish them if they do not do so when they are ten years old; and when they reach ten years, divide their beds.

Suspicion:

101. Suspicion is the blackest lie.

Sympathy:

102. Allah is not merciful to him who is not so to man-kind. He who is not kind to Allah's creation and to his own children, Allah will not be kind to him.

103. He who will do good to the needy, Allah will do good to him in this world and the next.

104. Whosoever visits a sick person, an angel calls from Heaven: "Be happy in the world and happy be your walk-ing; and take your habitation in Paradise.

Women:

105. A virtuous wife is a man's best treasure.

106. Do you beat your wife, as you would a slave? That must you not.

107. A Muslim must not hate his wife. If he is dis-pleased with one bad quality in her, let him be pleased with another, which is good.

108. The things which is lawful but disliked by Allah is divorce.

109. Do not prevent your women from coming to mosque; but their homes are preferable for them.

110. When a woman observes the five times of prayer, fasts during the month of *Ramadan* and is chaste and is not disobedient to her husband, then tell her to enter Paradise by whichever door she pleases.

World

111. The love of the world, is the root of all evils.

112. Wealth properly employed is a blessing; and a man may lawfully endeavour to increase it by honest means.

*   *   *   *   *

THE SECOND INFALLIBLE

THE DAUGHTER
OF
THE HOLY PROPHET

INSIDE VIEW OF THE PROPHET'S MOSQUE, MEDINA.

FATIMAH AZ-ZAHRA'
(Peace be on her)

Name: Fatimah
Title: az-Zahra'.
Agnomen: Ummu 'l-A'immah.
Father's name: Muhammad ibn `Abdillah.
Mother's name: Khadijah bint Khuwaylid.
Birth: Born in Mecca on Friday, 20th *Jumadi 'th-thaniyah* in the fifth year after the declaration of the Prophethood (615 AD).
Death: Died at the age of 18 in Medina on 14th *Jumadi-'l-ula 11 AH (632 AD)*; buried in the graveyard called Jannatu 'l-Baqi' in Medina.

HADRAT FATIMAH was the only daughter of the Holy Prophet and Hadrat Khadijah. The circumstances of her birth are described by Hadrat Khadijah as follows:

At the time of the birth of Hadrat Fatimah, I sent for my neighbouring Qurayshite women to assist me. They flatly refused, saying that I had betrayed them by supporting Muhammad. I was pertubed for a while, when, to my great surprise, I sighted four strange tall women with halos around them, approaching me.

Finding me dismayed, one of them addressed me thus, "O Khadijah! I am Sarah, the mother of Ishaq, and the other three are, Mary the mother of Christ, Asiyah the daughter of Muzahim, and Umm Kulthixm, the sister of Moses. We have all been commanded by God to put our nursing knowledge at your disposal." Saying this, all of them sat around me and rendered the services of midwifery till my daughter Fatimah was born.

The motherly blessings and affection received by Hadrat Fatimah were only for five years, after which Hadrat Khadijah left for her heavenly home. Hereafter the Holy Prophet brought her up.

Marriage

When Fatimah came of age, there came forward a number of aspirants to ask for her hand in marriage. The Holy Prophet was awaiting the Divine order in this respect, till Imam `Ali approached him and asked for her hand in marriage.

The Holy Prophet came to Hadrat Fatimah and asked, "My daughter! Do you consent to be wedded to `Ali, as I am so commanded by Allah? "

Hadrat Fatimah thereupon bowed her head in modesty. Umm Salamah narrates: "The face of Fatimah bloomed with joy and her silence was so suggestive and conspicuous that the Holy Prophet stood up reciting *Allahu Akbar'* (Allah is most great). Fatimah's silence is her acceptance."

On Friday, 1st *Dhi 'l-hijjah* 2 AH, the marriage ceremony took place. All the *Muhajirun* (Emigrants) and *Ansar* (Helpers) of Medina assembled in the mosque while Imam `Ali was seated before the Holy Prophet with all the ceremonious modesty of a bridegroom. The Holy Prophet first recited an eloquent sermon and then announced:

I have been commanded by Allah to get Fatimah
wedded to `Ali, and so I do hereby solemnize the
matrimony between `Ali and Fatimah on a dower
of four hundred *mithqal* of silver.

Then he asked Imam Ali, "Do you consent to it, O
Ali? " "Yes, I do, O Holy Prophet of Allah! " replied Imam
Ali. Then the Holy Prophet raised his hands to pray thus:
O my God! bless both of them, sanctify their progeny
and grant them the keys of Thy beneficence, Thy
treasures of wisdom and Thy genius; and let them
be a source of blessing and peace to my *ummah*.

Her children; Imam Hasan, Imam Husayn, Zaynab and
Umm Kulthum, are well-known for their piety, goodness
and generosity. Their strength of character and action
changed the course of history and fortified Islam which
otherwise would have been lost to mankind.

Her Ethical Attributes:

Hadrat Fatimah inherited the genius and wisdom,
the determination and will-power, the piety and sanctity,
the generosity and benevolence, the devotion and worship
of Allah, the self-sacrifice and hospitality, the forbearance
and patience, and the knowledge and nobility of disposition of her illustrious father, both in words and
deeds. "I often witnessed my mother," says Imam Husayn,
"absorbed in prayer from dusk to dawn." Her generosity
and compassion for the poor was such that no destitute
or beggar ever returned from her door unattended.

The Property of Fadak:

The Holy Prophet during his lifetime gave Hadrat
Fatimah a gift of very extensive farm land, known
as Fadak, which was documented in her name as her
absolute property.

The death of the Holy Prophet affected her very much and she was very sad and grief-stricken and wept her heart out crying all the time. She was confronted, after the demise of her father, with the deprivement of the rightful claim of leadership of her husband Imam Ali, and the usurpation of her inheritance, the Fadak. Throughout her life, she never spoke to those who had oppressed her and deprived her of her rightful claims. She requested that her oppressors should be kept away even from attending her funeral.

Her ill-wishers even resorted to physical violence. Once the door of her house was pushed on her, and the child she was carrying was hurt and the baby-boy was still born. Her house was set on fire.

Having been molested and stricken with grief, which crossed all limits of forbearance and endurance, she expressed her sorrows in an elegy composed by herself to mourn her father the Holy Prophet. A couplet of the elegy, with particular reference to her woeful plight, she expressed thus:

O my father! after your death I was subjected to such tortures and tyranny that if they had been inflicted on the `Day', it would have turned into `Night'.

Death

Hadrat Fatimah did not survive more than seventy-five days after the demise of her father. She breathed her last on the 14th Jumdi '1-ula 11 AH. Before her demise she bequeathed the following as her will to Imam `Ali:

1. O Ali, you will personally perform my funeral rites.

2. Those who have displeased me should not be allowed to attend my funeral.

3. My corpse should be carried to the graveyard at night.

Thus Imam `Ali, in compliance with her will, performed all the funeral rites and accompanied exclusively by her relatives and sons carried her at night to Jannatu 'l-Baqi `, where she was laid to rest and her wishes fulfilled.

The Holy Prophet said:

Whoever injures (bodily or sentimentally) Fatimah, injures me; and whoever injures me injures Allah; and whoever injures Allah practises unbelief. O Fatimah! If your wrath is incurred, it incurs the wrath of Allah; and if you are happy, it makes Allah happy too.

M. H. Shakir writes:

Fatimah, the only daughter of the Holy Prophet of Islam, was born in Mecca on 20th *Jumadi 'th-thaniyah* 18 BH.

The good and noble lady Khadijah and the Apostle of Allah bestowed all their natural love, care and devotion on their lovable and only child Fatimah, who in her turn was extremely fond of her parents.

The Princess of the House of the Prophet, was very intelligent, accomplished and cheerful. Her sermons, poems and sayings serve, as an index to her strength of character and nobility of mind.

Her virtues gained her the title "Our Lady of Light". She was tall, slender and endowed with great beauty, which caused her to be called "az-Zahra' " (the Lady of Light). She was called az-Zahra' because her light used to shine among those in Heaven.

After arriving in Medina, she was married to `Ali, in the first year Hijrah, and she gave birth to three sons and two daughters.

Her children, Hasan, Husayn, Zaynab and Umm Kulthum are well-known for their piety, goodness and generosity. Their strength of character and actions changed the course of history.

The Holy Prophet said, "Fatimah is a peace of my heart". He would go out to receive his daughter whenever she came from her husband's house. Every morning on his way to the Mosque, he would pass by Fatimah's house and say, *"as-Salamu `alaykum ya ahla Bayti 'n-nubuwwah wa ma`dani 'r-risalah "* (Peace be on you O the Household of Prophethood and the Source of Messengership).

Fatimah is famous and acknowledged as the "Sayyidatu nisa '1-`alamin" (Leader of all the women of the world for all times) because the Prophethood of Muhammad would not have been everlasting without her. The Prophet is the perfect example for men, but could not be so for women. For all the verses revealed in the Holy Qur'an for women, Fatimah is the perfect model, who translated every verse into action. In her lifetime, she was a complete woman, being Daughter, Wife and Mother at the same time.

Muhammad during his lifetime, gave Fatimah a gift of very extensive farm lands, famous as Fadak, which were documented in her name, as her absolute personal property.

An heiress to the remainder of her mother's wealth, a princess who was the only daughter of the Holy Prophet who was also a ruler, a lady whose husband was the con queror of Arab tribes and second only to her father in rank and position, Fatimah could have led a luxurious life. But in spite of her wealth and possessions, she worked, dressed, ate and lived very simply. She was very generous; and none who came to her door, went away empty handed.

Many times she gave away her all and herself went without food.

As a daughter, she loved her parents so much, that she won their love and regard to such an extent that the Holy Prophet used to rise, whenever she came near him.

As a wife, she was very devoted. She never asked `Ali for anything in her whole life.

As a mother, she cared for and brought up wonderful children; they have left their marks on the face of the world, which time will not be able to eraze.

The death of the Apostle, affected her very much and she was very sad and grief-striken and wept her heart out crying all the time.

Unfortunately, after the death of the Prophet, the Government confiscated her famous land of Fadak and gave it to the State. Fatimah was pushed behind her home door (when they attacked the house of `Ali and took him to force him accept the caliphate of Abu Bakr), so that the child, she was carrying was hurt and the baby-boy Muhsin was still born. Her house was set on fire by the Government.

The tragedy of her father's death and the unkindness of her father's followers, were too much for the good, gentle and sensitive lady and she breathed her last on 14th Jumdi 'l-ula 11 AH, exactly seventy-five days after the death of her father, the Holy Prophet of Islam.

Fatimah died in the prime of her life at the age of eighteen, and was buried in Jannatu 'l-Baqi', Medina.

*   *   *   *   *

قَالَتِ الصِّدِّيقَةُ الكُبْرى عليها السَّلَامُ :

... فَجَعَلَ اللهُ الإِيمانَ تَطْهِيرًا لَكُمْ مِنَ الشَّرْكِ، وَالصَّلاَةَ تَنْزِيهاً لَكُمْ عَنِ الْكِبْرِ،
وَالزَّكَاةَ تَزْكِيَةً لِلنَّفْسِ وَنَمَاءً فِي الرِّزْقِ، وَالصِّيَامَ تَثْبِيتاً لِلإِخْلاَصِ، وَالحَجَّ تَشْيِيداً لِلدِّينِ،
وَالْعَدْلَ تَنْسِيقاً لِلْقُلُوبِ، وَ طَاعَتَنَا نِظَاماً لِلْمِلَّةِ، وَ إِمَامَتَنَا أَمَاناً مِنَ الْفُرْقَةِ، وَالْجِهَادَ عِزّا
لِلإِسْلاَم وَذُلاًّ لأَهْلِ الْكُفْرِ وَالنَّفَاقِ (...) وَالأَمْرَ بِالْمَعْرُوفِ وَالنَّهْيَ عَنِ الْمُنْكَرِ مَصْلَحَةً
لِلعَامَّةِ، وَ بِرَّ الْوَالِدَيْنِ وِقَايَةً مِنَ السُّخْطِ، وَ صِلَةَ الأَرْحَامِ مَنْسَأَةً فِي الْعُمْرِ (...) وَالنَّهْيَ عَنْ
شُرْبِ الْخَمْرِ تَنْزِيهاً عَنِ الرِّجْسِ (...) وَ حَرَّمَ اللهُ الشِّرْكَ إِخْلاَصاً لَهُ بِالرُّبُوبِيَّةِ (فَاتَّقُوا اللهَ حَقَّ
تُقَاتِهِ وَلاَ تَمُوتُنَّ إِلاَّ وَأَنْتُمْ مُسْلِمُونَ.) (آل عمران، ٣/١٠٢)

Allah has made faith *(Iman)* [the means] to purify one from polytheism *(shirk);* and [made] prayer *(salat)* to guard one from arrogance; and [prescribed] alms *(zakat)* to chasten one's self and increase one's sustenance; and [prescribed] the fast *(sawm)* to strengthen sincere devotion [to Allah]; and [prescribed] the pilgrimage *(hajj) to* elevate the religion *(din);* and [enjoined] justice *(adl)* to harmonize the hearts; and [enjoined] obedience to us *(A hlu 'l-bayt)* to organize the Islamic community *(millah);* and our Leadership *(imamah)* as a trust to avoid disunity; and [prescribed] holy war *(jihad)* to honour Islam and denounce the unbelievers and hypocrites; and the bidding of good *(amr bi 'l-ma'ruf)* and forbidding of evil *(nahy ani 'l-munkar)* for the benefit of the people in general; and kindness to parents as a shield against the anger [of Allah]; and strengthening one's ties with near kin to prolong [one's] life: .. . and the forbiddance of alcoholic drink to guard one from filth; and Allah has prohibited polytheism for the sincere devotion to His Divinity; so [O you who believe!] *fear Allah as you should, and* [see that] you *die not but as Muslims* [3:102]. (An excerpt from a lengthy speech delivered at the Mosque of the Prophet [at Medina] in defence of her right of inheritance).

TWELVE APOSTOLIC IMAMS

The Apostle of Allah said:
After me there will be Twelve Imams or Caliphs:
and
The first of us is Muhammad;
The last of us is Muhammad;
In between us are Muhammad;
And all of us are Muhammad;
For all of us are from One *Nur* (Light).

THE IMAMS

The Holy Prophet Muhammad (peace be on him and his progeny) said: "I shall be succeeded by twelve religious leaders, all of whom will be of Qurayshite origin." (al-Bukhari, *as-Sahih*)

The twelve Imams are these sacred personages and spiritual leaders about whom the Holy Prophet had prophesied. Pointing them out as the source and means of guidance for mankind, the Holy Prophet remarked: "So long as my twelve successors will continue to govern, this religion (Islam) will exist (in this world)." (Abu Dawud, *as-Sunan*)

On a request from his well-known companion, Jabir ibn Abdillah al-Ansari, the Holy Prophet explained the names of his twelve successors thus: "They are my twelve successors, O Jabir, who will come after me. First of them will be Ali, who will be followed, one after the other, by Hasan, Husayn, Ali ibn al-Husayn, Muhammad ibn `Ali, Ja'far ibn Muhammad, Musa ibn Ja'far, Ali ibn Musa, Muhammad ibn `Ali, `Ali ibn Muhammad, Hasan ibn Ali and lastly by Muhammad al-Mahdi, al-Qa'im (peace be on them)."

47

LINEAL CHART OF THE TWELVE APOSTOLIC IMAMS

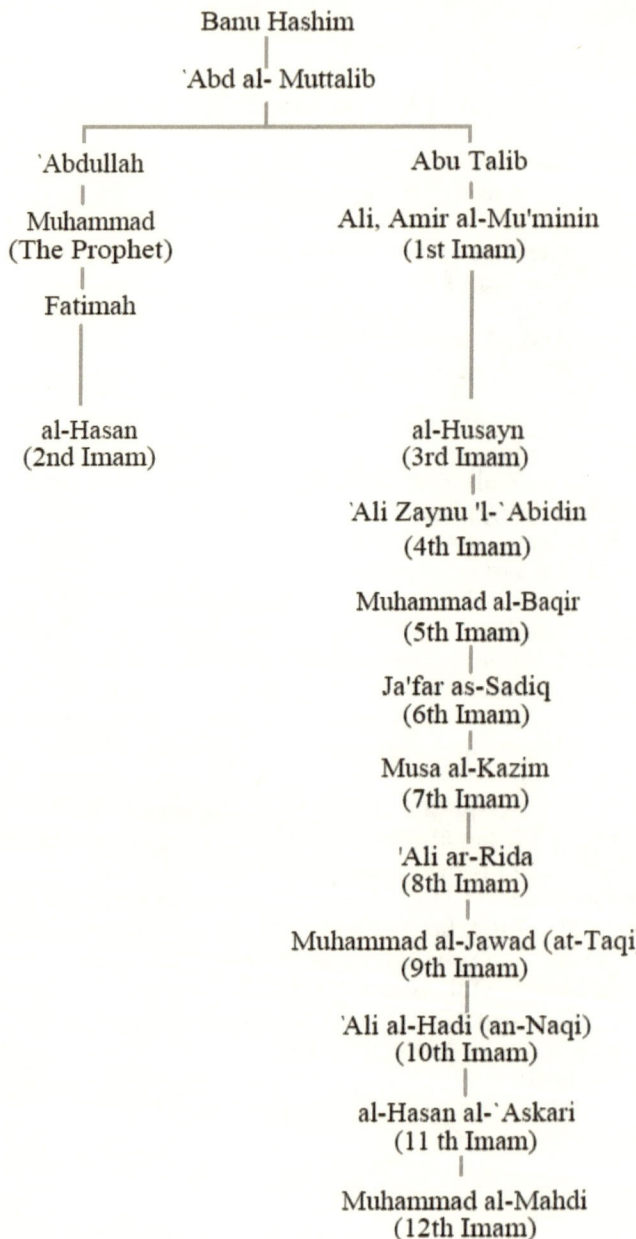

Banu Hashim

`Abd al- Muttalib

`Abdullah

Muhammad
(The Prophet)

Fatimah

al-Hasan
(2nd Imam)

Abu Talib

Ali, Amir al-Mu'minin
(1st Imam)

al-Husayn
(3rd Imam)

`Ali Zaynu 'l-`Abidin
(4th Imam)

Muhammad al-Baqir
(5th Imam)

Ja'far as-Sadiq
(6th Imam)

Musa al-Kazim
(7th Imam)

'Ali ar-Rida
(8th Imam)

Muhammad al-Jawad (at-Taqi)
(9th Imam)

`Ali al-Hadi (an-Naqi)
(10th Imam)

al-Hasan al-`Askari
(11 th Imam)

Muhammad al-Mahdi
(12th Imam)

THE THIRD INFALLIBLE

THE FIRST IMAM

THE HOLY SHRINE OF AMIR AL-MU'MININ 'ALI IBN
ABI TALIB (A.S.), AN-NAJAF AL-ASHRAF (IRAQ).

`ALI IBN ABI TALIB, AMIR AL-MU'MININ
(Peace be on him)

Name: Ali.

Title: al-Murtada.

Agnomen. Abu. 'l-Hasan.

Father's name: Abu Talib ibn `Abd al-Muttalib.

Mother's name: Fatimah bint Asad.

Birth: In the Holy Ka'bah in Mecca on Friday, 13th *Rajab* 23 B H.

Death: Died at the age of 63, in Kufah (Iraq) on Monday, 21st *Ramadan* 40 AH; murdered by an assassin who mortally wounded him with a poisoned sword in the mosque of Kufah during the morning prayer on 19th *Ramadan;* buried in an-Najaf al-Ashraf (Iraq).

IMAM ALI was the cousin of our Holy Prophet. He was born in the Sacred House (Ka'bah). Providence alone had a hand in bringing his mother towards the Ka'bah. When his mother came to Ka'bah, she felt weighed down by intense pain of pregnancy. She knelt down before the Holy Structure and prayed humbly to God. `Abbas ibn

51

Abd al-Muttalib, saw Ali's mother praying to God. No sooner had she raised her head from supplication, then the wall of the Sacred House split by a solemn miracle. Fatimah entered the Ka'bah and that portion returned to its normal position. `Abbas and his companions flocked at the gate of the Sacred House which was locked, and tried to open it, but in vain. They then decided to give it up, considering the miraculous nature of the event and the Divine Will in action. The news of this miraculous incident soon spread like wild fire in Mecca.

`Ali was born within the Ka'bah with his eyes closed and his body in humble prostration before the Almighty. Fatimah stayed in the Ka'bah for three days and as the fourth day approached she stepped out, carrying her gem in her arms. To her great surprise, she found the Holy Prophet awaiting to receive the newly-born child in his anxious arms. Imamate feeling the subtle touch of prophethood, Ali opened his eyes and saluted the Divine Prophet: *"as-Salamu alayka ya Rasula 'llah"* (Peace be on you, O Messenger of Allah).

'Ali's birth in the Ka'bah is unique in the history of the world. Neither a prophet nor a Divine saint was ever blessed with such an honour.

He was brought up under the care and affection of the Holy Prophet. As Ali says: "The Holy Prophet brought me up in his own arms and fed me with his own morsel. I followed him wherever he went like a baby-camel following its mother. Each day a new aspect of his character would beam out of his noble person and I would accept it and follow it as a command." *(Nahju 'l-balaghah)*

Ten years in the company of the Holy Prophet had kept him so close and inseparable, that he was one with him in character, knowledge, self-sacrifice, forbearance, bravery, kindness, generosity, oratory and eloquence.

From his very infancy, he prostrated before God along with the Holy Prophet. As he himself said: "I was the first to pray to God along with the Holy Prophet. "

"Ali preserved in the footsteps of the Holy Prophet," says al-Mas'udi, "all along his childhood." Allah created him pure and holy and kept him steadfast on the right path. Though 'Ali is undisputably the first to embrace Islam when the Holy Prophet called upon his listeners to do so, yet by the very fact that since his infancy he was brought up by the Holy Prophet and followed him in every action and deed including prostration before Allah, he can be said to be born a Muslim, just like the Holy Prophet himself.

'Ali, at all times, accompanied the Holy Prophet to help and protect him from his enemies. He used to write down the verses of the Holy Qur'an and discuss them with the Prophet as soon as they were revealed by the Holy Messenger, the Gabriel. He was so closely associated with the Holy Prophet that as soon as a verse was revealed to him during the day or night, Ali was the first to hear it.

The Holy Prophet has said of `Ali:

O `Ali, you are my brother in this world as well as in the Hereafter.

I am the city of knowledge and 'Ali is the gate.

Nobody knows 'Ali except Allah and I.

Nobody know me except Allah and `Ali.

If you want to see the knowledge of Adam, the piety of Noah, the devotion of Abraham, the awe of Moses, and the service and abstinence of Christ, look at the bright face of `Ali.

When the Holy Prophet reached Yathrib (Medina) and met his followers who had come from Mecca at his call, he immediately appointed for each such followers a person from the people of Yathrib known as Ansar (Helpers), who had accepted his prophethood, to be a brother to him. His appointment of brothers was a great act of help for the refugees known as *Muhajirun* (Emigrants), who left their home and come to Yathrib. He made brothers of people who followed the same trade so that the *Muhajirun* could be usefully employed immediately. While the Prophet was appointing an *Ansar* a brother to a *Muhajirun*, `Ali who was present there, was not appointed as a brother to any *Ansar*. On being questioned as to why he had not appointed a brother for Ali, the Prophet said: "He shall be a brother to me. "

The character and calibre of `Ali as judged by al-Mas'udi is, "If the glorious name of being the first Muslim, a comrade of the Prophet in exile, his faithful compan ion in the struggle for faith, his intimate associate in life, and his kinsman; if a true knowledge of the spirit of his teachings and of the Book; if self-abnegation and practice of justice; if honesty, purity, and love of truth; if a knowledge of law and science, constitute a claim to pre-eminence, then all must regard `Ali as the foremost Muslim. We shall search in vain to find, either among his predecessors (save one) or among his successors, those attributes. "

Gibbon says: "The birth, the alliance, the character of `Ali which exalted him above the rest of his country-men, might justify his claim to the vacant throne of Arabia. The son of Abu Talib was in his own right the chief of Banu Hashim and the hereditary prince or guardian of the city and the Ka'bah."

" `Ali had the qualifications of a poet, a soldier, and a saint; his wisdom still breathes in a collection of moral and religious sayings; and every antagonist, in the combats of the tongue or of the sword, was subdued by his eloquence and valour. From the first hour of his mission to the last rites of his funeral, the Apostle was never forsaken by a generous friend, whom he delighted to name his brother, his vicegerent, and the faithful Aaron of a second Moses."

Marriage:

Under Divine instruction, the Apostle of Allah married his beloved daughter Fatimah to Ali, though others vainly tried for her hand.

Among their children, Imam Hasan, Imam Husayn, Zaynab and Umm Kulthum have left their marks on the history of the world.

After the death of Hadrat Fatimah, `Ali married Ummu '1-Banin. `Abbas was born out of this wedlock and was so handsome that, he was fondly called Qamar Banu Hashim. He personified loyalty and bravery and proved it in the battlefield at Karbala'.

Death

In the 40th year of Hijrah, in the small hours of the morning of 19th *Ramadan,* Ali was struck with a poisoned sword by a Kharijite while offering his prayers in the mosque of Kufah. (See photo on p.56)

The Lion of God, the most brave-hearted and fentle Muslim that ever lived began his glorious life with devotion to Allah and His Apostle and ended it in the service of Islam.

وَلاَ تَقُولُوا لِمَنْ يُقْتَلُ فِي سَبِيلِ أللهِ أَمْوَاتٌ بَلْ أَحْيَآءٌ وَلكِنْ لاَ تَشْعُرُونَ. (البقرة، ٢/١٥٤)

And do not speak of those who are slain in Allah's way as dead; nay they are alive but you do not perceive. (Qur'an, 2:154)

INTERIOR VIEW OF THE MOSQUE OF KUFAH AND
THE DOME OF MUSLIM IBN `AQIL, KUFAH (IRAQ).

THE IMAMS AND LEADERS OF ISLAM
(By al-`Allamah at-Tabataba'i)

The previous discussions lead us to the conclusion that in Islam, after the death of the Holy Prophet, there has continuously existed and will continue to exist with in the Islamic community *(ummah),* an Imam (a leader chosen by God). Numerous prophetic *hadiths* have been transmitted in Shi'ism concerning the description of the Imams, their number, the fact that they are all of the Quraysh and of the Household of the Prophet, and the fact that the promised Mahdi is among them and the last of them. Also, there are definitive words of the Prophet concerning the Imamate of `Ali and his being the first Imam and also definitive utterances of the Prophet and Ali concerning the Imamate of the Second Imam. In the same way the Imams before have left definitive statements concerning the Imamate of those who were to come after them. According to these utterances contained in Twelve-Imam Shi`ite sources the Imams are twelve in number and their holy names are as follows: (1) `Ali ibn Abi Talib; (2) al-Hasan ibn 'Ali; (3) al-Husayn ibn 'Ali; (4) 'Ali ibn al- Husayn; (5) Muhammad ibn `Ali; (6) Ja'far ibn Muhammad; (7) Musa ibn Ja'far; (8) `Ali ibn Musa; (9) Muhammad ibn Ali; (10) `Ali ibn Muhammad; (11) al-Hasan ibn 'Ali; and (12) the Mahdi.

The First Imam:

Amir al-Mu'minin, `Ali (upon whom be peace) was the son of Abu Talib, the Shaykh of the Banu Hashim. Abu Talib was the uncle and guardian of the Holy Prophet and the person who had brought the Prophet to his house and raised him like his own son. After the Prophet was chosen for his prophetic mission. Abu Talib continued to support him and repelled from him the evil that came from the infidels among the Arabs and especially the Quraysh.

According to well-known traditional accounts, `Ali was born ten years before the commencement of the prophetic misssion of the Prophet. When six years old, as a result of femine in and around Mecca, he was requested by the Prophet to leave his father's house and come to the house of his cousin, the Prophet. There he was placed directly under the guardianship and custody of the Holy Prophet.

A few years later, when the Prophet was endowed with the Divine Gift of prophecy and for the first time received the Divine Revelation in the cave of Hira', as he left the cave to return to town and his own house he met 'Ali on the way. He told him what had happened and `Ali accepted the new faith. Again in a gathering when the   Holy Prophet had brought his relatives together and invited them to accept his religion, he said the first person to accept his call would be his vicegerent and inheritor and deputy. The only person to rise from his place and accept the faith was Ali and the Prophet accepted his declaration of faith. Therefore, `Ali was the first man in Islam to accept the faith and is the first among the followers of the Prophet to have never worshipped other than the One God.

Ali was always in the company of the Prophet until the Prophet emigrated from Mecca to Medina. On the night of the emigration to Medina *(hijrah)* when the infidels had surrounded the house of the Prophet and were determined to invade the house at the end of the night and cut him to pieces while he was in bed. Ali slept in place of the Prophet while the Prophet left the house and set out for Medina. After the departure of the Prophet, according to his wish `Ali gave back to the people the trusts and charges that they had left with the Prophet. Then he went to Medina with his mother, the daughter of the Prophet, and two other women. In Medina also `Ali was constantly in the company of the Prophet in private and in public. The Prophet gave Fatimah, his sole, beloved daughter from Khadijah, to `Ali as his wife and when the Prophet was creating bonds of brotherhood among his companions, he selected `Ali as his brother.

`Ali was present in all the wars in which the Prophet participated, except the battle of Tabuk when he was ordered to stay in Medina in place of the Prophet. He did not retreat in any battle nor did he turn his face away from any enemy. He never disobeyed the Prophet, so that the Prophet said: " `Ali is never separated from the Truth nor the Truth from Ali."

On the day of the death of the Prophet, Ali was thirty-three years old. Although he was foremost in religious virtues and the most outstanding among the companions of the Prophet, he was pushed aside from the caliphate on the claim that he was too young and that he had many enemies among the people because of the blood of the polytheists he had spilled in the wars fought alongside the Prophet. Therefore, `Ali was almost completely cut off from public affairs. He retreated to his house where he began to train competent individuals in the Divine sciences and in this way he passed the twenty-five years of the caliphate of the first three caliphs who (came to power after the Prophet; the first by election of few Muslims; the second appointed by the first; and the third, chosen out of six unequal candidates nominated by the second caliph. . .?!). When the third caliph was killed, people gave their allegiance to him and he was chosen as Caliph.

During his caliphate of nearly four years and nine months, `Ali followed, exactly, the way of the Prophet and gave his caliphate the form of a spiritual movement and renewal and began many different types of reforms. Naturally, these reforms were against the interests of certain parties that sought their own benefit. As a result, a group of the companions (foremost among whom were Talhah and az-Zubayr, who also gained the support of 'A'ishah, and especially Mu'awiyah) made a pretext of the death of the third caliph to raise their heads in opposition and began to revolt and rebel against `Ali.

In order to quell the civil strife and sedition, `Ali fought successfully a war near Basrah known as the "Battle of the Camel," against Talhah and az-Zubayr in which 'A'ishah, "the Mother of the Faithful," was also involved. He fought another war against Mu'awiyah on the border of Iraq and Syria which lasted for a year and a half and is famous as the "Battle of Siffin". He also fought the Khawarij at Nahrawan, in a battle known as the "Battle of Nahrawan". Therefore, most of the days of `Ali's caliphate were spent in overcoming internal opposition. Finally, in the morning of the 19th *Ramadan* in the year 40 AH, while praying in the mosque of Kufah, he was wounded by one of the Khawarij and died as a martyr during the night of the 21st.

According to the testimony of friend and foe alike, 'Ali had no shortcomings from the point of view of human perfection. And in the Islamic virtues he was a perfect example of the upbringing and training given by the Holy Prophet. The discusssions that have taken place concerning his personality and the books written on this subject by Shiites, Sunnis and members of other religions, as well as the simply curious outside any distinct religious bodies, are hardly equalled in the case of any other personality in history. In science and knowledge `Ali was the most learned of the companions of the Prophet, and of Muslims in general. In his learned discourses he was the first in Islam to open the door for logical demonstration and proof and to discuss the "divine science" or metaphysics *(ma'arif-e ilahiyyah)*. He spoke concerning the esoteric aspect of the Qur'an and devised Arabic grammar in order to preserve the Qur'an's form of expression. He was the most eloquent Arab in speech (as has been mentioned in the first part of this book).

The courage of `Ali was proverbial. In all the wars in which he participated during the lifetime of the Holy Prophet, and also afterward, he never displayed fear or anxiety. Although in many battles such as those of Uhud, Hunayn, Khaybar and Khandaq, the aides to the Prophet and the Muslim army trembled in fear or dispersed and fled, he never turned back to the enemy. Never did a warrior or soldier engage Ali in battle and come out of it alive. Yet, with full chivalry he would never slay a weak enemy nor pursue those who fled. He would not engage in surprise attacks or in turning streams of water upon the enemy. It has been definitely established historically that in the Battle of Khaybar in the attack against the fort he reached the ring of the door and with sudden motion tore off the door and cast it away. Also, on the day when Mecca was conquered the Prophet ordered the idols to be broken. The idol "Hubal" was the largest idol in Mecca, a giant stone statue placed on the top of the Ka'bah. Following the command of the Holy Prophet, `Ali placed his feet on the Prophet's shoulders, climbed to the top of the Ka'bah, pulled "Hubal" from its place and cast it down.

`Ali was also without equal in religious asceticism and the worship of God. In answer to some who had

complained of Ali's anger toward them, the Holy Prophet
said: "Do not reproach 'Ali for he is in a state of Divine
ecstasy and bewilderment." Abu 'd-Darda', one of the
companions, one day saw the body of 'Ali in one of the
palm plantations of Medina lying on the ground as stiff
as wood. He went to `Ali's house to inform his noble
wife, the daughter of the Prophet, and to express his
condolences. The daughter of the Prophet said: "My
cousin (`Ali) has not died. Rather, in fear of God he
has fainted. This condition overcomes him often."

There are many stories told of `Ali's kindness to the
lowly, compassion for the needy and the poor, and generosity and munificence toward those in misery and poverty.
`Ali spent all that he earned to help the poor and the
needy, and himself lived in the strictest and simplest manner. 'Ali loved agriculture and spent much of his time
digging wells, planting trees and cultivating fields. But
all the fields that he cultivated or wells that he built he
gave in endowment *(waqf)* to the poor. His endowments,
known as the "alms of `Ali," had the noteworthy income
of twenty-four thousand gold dinars towards the end of
his life. (*Shi'ite Islam*)

M. A. Shakir writes:

'Ali is the son of Abu Talib and cousin of the Apostle
of Allah.

Birth

He was born in the House of God, the Ka'bah on 13th
Rajab 23 years before Hijrah.

On the death of `Abdu 1-Muttalib, Abu Talib was ap-
pointed the guardian of Muhammad and was charged with
the responsibility of bringing him up. Muhammad and 'Ali

grew up in the same house. The Prophet was considerably older and he looked after and trained 'Ali with great love and care.

The Apostle of Allah said that he and `Ali were two pieces of the same *Nur* (Light).

Successor and Caliph

According to the Holy Qur'an, Prophets and Apostolic Imams are chosen by Allah and not elected, selected, nominated or appointed by men.

1. When under Divine instructions the Prophet invited fourty Arab chieftains and delivered the message of Islam, he proclaimed Ali as his Successor and Caliph.

2. When the Holy Prophet of Islam was returning to Medina after his last pilgrimage to Mecca in 11 AH, he, under Divine instruction, stopped at Ghadir Khumm and in the midst of about 124,000 Muslims, he officially and finally proclaimed 'Ali as his Successor and Caliph.

(Besides these two occasions, the Holy Prophet has on hundreds occasions, either directly or indirectly, appointed Ali as his Successor and Caliph.)

Happy Days

The infant Ali passed very happy days in the laps of his mother Fatimah bint Asad, father Abu Talib and cousin Muhammad.

Under love, care and happiness, 'Ali flowered into a handsome, eloquent, strong and courageous young boy of thirteen.

At this time Muhammad started preaching Islam. Naturally, 'Ali was the first to declare his belief in Allah and His Apostle.

Persecution

Gone were the days of tranquillity and peace. The unbelievers started persecuting the Prophet in numerous ways, for no fault other than that of delivering to them the message of God. 'Ali helped and supported the Prophet whenever necessary.

The unbelievers made the boys and the riffraffs of Mecca abuse the Holy Prophet and pelt stones at him. Loyal and brave 'Ali always defended the Prophet. With his strong fists, he gave the rascals severe beatings, after that none of them dare molest the Prophet.

Hijrah (Emigration)

In Mecca, life for the believers and the Apostle became unbearable   owing to the cruelties and persecution of the unbelievers; so the Holy Prophet decided to emigrate to Medina.

On the night of his departure from Mecca, the Holy Prophet asked `Ali to sleep in his place on his bed, so he could leave for Medina without the unbelievers having any knowledge of his absence. Though 'Ali knew that the house was surrounded with forty armed enemies, he dauntlessly slept the whole night and said that he had never slept better. The Holy Prophet reached Medina safely and soon after, `Ali joined the Apostle at Medina.

Warrior

'Ali executed every order, command and injunction of the Holy Qur'an and the Apostle, as it should be done and none was his equal.

Badr

The idolaters of Mecca would not allow Islam to grow
and spread in peace.

Abu Sufyan, the chieftain of the Umayyad tribe, a
bitter enemy of the Holy Prophet and Islam marched
to Medina at the head of one-thousand well-armed and
trained fighters with the intention of killing the Apostle
of Allah and the believers.

The Holy Prophet collected his small band of three-
hundred and thirteen faithful followers. The defence was
made up of ill-equipped fighters, including young boys
and old men.

Instead of waiting for the attackers, the Prophet
decided to meet them at a little distance from Medina
at a place called Badr (150 Km from Medina).

The fighting was fast and furious and the unbelievers
were defeated. `Ali made a name for himself for his brav-
ery. It was his sword that routed the enemy.

Uhud

Next year Abu Sufyan came again with 10,000 men.
The Prophet met him at Uhud with a 1,000 believers who
were posted at various strategic places of defence.

A few Muslims were given specific instruction not
to leave their position, no matter what happened.

The battle began and with the help of Allah, the
believers inflicted heavy losses on the enemy, who began
to flee. In spite of the strict instructions of the Holy
Prophet, a few Muslims deserted their post and ran after
the enemy to loot.

Khalid ibn al-Walid, one of the officers of Abu Sufyan,
seeing the position occupied by Muslims undefended,

attacked the believers. Many believers were killed including Hamzah, the brave uncle of the Prophet and winning fight began to become a losing one. `Ali came to the rescue (of the life of the Prophet) and beat off the attack.

After Hamzah and Ja'far, 'Ali was the flag bearer of Islam. Ali was the only commander of the Holy Prophet during his life and no other person was given the command of the Prophet's armies in the battles in which the Holy Prophet was himself taking part.

The wife of Abu Sufyan, cut open the liver of Hamzah and drank his blood. Then she made a necklace of the ears and noses of the martyrs and wore it round her neck.

When the Muslims returned to Medina to weep and mourn for their dead, the Apostle ordered that the mourning of Hamzah be observed before the mourning of their own dead.

Khandaq

The battle of Khandaq took place because Abu Sufyan collected many infidel tribes against the Prophet and invaded Medina. To make Medina safe the Prophet ordered a trench *(khandaq)* to be dug around a part of the City, and therefore this battle is called the Battle of the Trench. In this battle the enemy warrior Amr ibn `Abdawad challenged the Muslims to a single combat. All the companions of the Prophet were present, yet none stirred except `Ali. But Muhammad restrained him. The challenge was repeated for the second time, even then no one moved to accept it but Ali Again the Apostle stopped him. When they were challenged for the third time and again there was a silence from all, and again 'Ali offered to face `Amr, the Prophet gave him the permission. The Lion of Allah jumped to the battlefield and accepted the challenge.

The Holy Prophet of Islam said:

Total Iman(faith) is now going to fight total kufr
(disbelief) and one stroke of Ali's sword is better
than all the prayers and worship of those in heaven
and earth.

'Ali with one stroke of his sword, Dhu 'l-Faqar, killed
the warrior. In the general encounter the enemy was
defeated.

Khaybar

The Jews of Khaybar breached their agreement with
the Prophet and started harassing and killing the Muslims.

An army led by the Apostle surrounded the fortresses
of Khaybar. 'Ali was at Medina because of pain in his eyes.

For many days, the Muslims attacked the fort but
were unsuccessful. After some days the Holy Prophet
declared:

Tomorrow, I will give the flag to one who will not
run away. He will attack repeatedly and Allah will
crown him with victory. Allah and the Apostle are
his friends and he is their friend.

Next morning soon after prayers, a horseman came
galloping, a cloud of dust flying behind him. It was 'Ali
and when he dismounted, Muhammad asked him about
his eyes. When 'Ali said that they were still paining, the
Prophet applied his saliva. The pain vanished and 'Ali
said that his vision had never been better.

Muhammad gave the flag of Islam to Ali and prayed
for him. 'Ali dauntlessly marched to the fort.

Marhab, the brave enemy warrior, came out to meet
'Ali in a single combat. According to the Arab custom,
Marhab talked of his deeds of bravery and said that his
mother called him Marhab (frightful). 'Ali retorted that

his mother called him Haydar (Furious Lion).

'Ali cut Marhab into two pieces and the fort of Khaybar was conquered by *Yadu 'llah* (Ali).

Statesman

At Hudaybiyyah, Ali was asked by the Holy Prophet to draft and write the peace treaty.

On the occasion of Mubahilah with the Christians of Najran, the Holy Prophet asked 'Ali to give them the terms of settlement.

'Ali is the founder of the land revenue system which protected the rights of the tillers of the soil. He gave the world this system, for it was unknown before.

'Ali is the father of the Arabic Grammar. He gave the language its grammar.

The Chapter of Repentance (*al-Bara'ah* or *at -Tawbah*) had to be recited to the people of Mecca, Abu Bakr offered to do so and started on his way. The angel Gabriel came with a message from God, asking the Prophet to recall Abu Bakr and to go himself or to send a person like him. As the Holy Prophet could not go, he decided to send 'Ali and 'Ali represented the Holy Prophet to carry this Chapter to the Quraysh.

Marriage

Under Divine instruction, the Apostle of Allah married his beloved daughter Fatimah to 'Ali.

Among their children, Imam Hasan, Imam Husayn, Zaynab and Umm Kulthum have left their marks on the history of the world.

By his other wife, Ummu 'l-Banin, Allah gave him Abbas who was so handsome that he was fondly called

Qamar Bani Hashim (The Moon of Banu Hashim) and he personified his loyalty and bravery in the battlefield of Karbala'.

Hadith

When the Apostle led his army to Tabuk, he left `Ali in charge of Medina as his Deputy, Vicegerent and Caliph. On this occasion the Apostle of Allah said:

Ali's position with me is the same as Harun's was with Musa, with only this difference that there will be no prophet after me.

He (the Prophet) said:

I leave behind Two Precious Things; one is the Holy Qur'an and the other are my descendants. Hold fast to them both, then you will not go astray.

And he (the Prophet) again said:

I, `Ali, Fatimah, Hasan and Husayn are from the same *Nur* (Light).

But like the ever-shifting sands, the people of Arabia disregarded the sayings of the Holy Prophet and introduced innovations which irretrievably divided the Muslims.

Death of the Prophet

During the last days of the month of *Safar,* the Prophet of Islam was very ill. The Companions saw that the Apostle would soon pass away.

Abu Bakr

The Arabs (some of the *Ansar* and at the end of the meeting three of the *Muhajirun*) immediately collected in the Saqifah to appoint a caliph (while the holy body of the Prophet was still unburied) ; and finally appointed Abu Bakr as caliph in 11 AH.

Banu Hashim and the true believers could not join the meeting at the Saqifah as they could not leave their ailing Prophet, who passed away on 28th Safar 11 AH. While the meetings were going on, the Banu Hashim and the true believers had to perform their sacred duty of burying the Apostle of Allah (after all, the Prophet had already appointed `Ali as his caliph).

The reason for this astounding happening was the desire to rule the State. In course of about eighty battles, there was not a tribe or family, whose members were not killed by Ali in *jihad,* though Allah and His Apostle had chosen Ali as the successor and caliph.

When Abu Bakr became the caliph, he said that now he was charged with the cares of the Government, though he was not the best among them. As death approached him, he nominated `Umar as his successor and caliph in 13 A H.

`Umar

For about ten years `Umar was the caliph, and before his death, he nominated a group of six (unequal in rank and knowledge) to select, under force, one (among the six) as a caliph, and if they fail they should be killed. Imam `Ali being one of the six nominated persons, having refused to abide with the group's condition to rule on the footsteps of the two passed caliphs (Abu Bakr and `Umar), the group then selected `Uthman, who was from the tribe of Umayyad, as the third caliph in 23 AH.

`Uthman

When `Uthman became the caliph, his near kin the

Umayyads, became the actual rulers of the Islamic terri-
tories. The caliphate of `Uthman with the governors he
had like Mu'awiyah, son of Abu Sufyan (the first and long-
lived enemy of Islam), was first appointed by `Umar as the
governor of Syria, and was responsible for the murders
of Imam 'Ali and Imam Hasan. Mu'awiya's son Yazid
butchered Imam Husayn (the grandson of the Prophet)
at Karbala'. And like al-Walid ibn `Uqbah ibn Abi Mu'ayt,
the governor of Kufah; and Abdullah ibn Abi Sarh, the
governor of Egypt, and above all, his close councillor
and vizier Marwan ibn al-Hakam he had, the affairs of
the caliphate reached to such an extent that led the
Islamic *ummah* to revolt against `Uthman and killed him
in 35 AH.

'Ali

Among sufferings and chaos, the Muslims clamoured
to elect 'Ali as the successor of the Holy Prophet and
caliph of Allah.

Looking to the condition of the society, how everyone was running after this world, `Ali at first refused to
accept the responsibility of the State, but on the third
day with great reluctance, he agreed to take up the charge
and to accept their oath of allegiance as a caliph.

Following the footsteps of the Holy Prophet, 'Ali
established the Islamic tolerance and justice, brotherhood and goodness. He re-lit the torch of Islamic learning
and progress.

Ali's famous sermons and lectures given from the
minbar (pulpit) of the mosque of Kufah and on other
occasions, have been published in a book called *Nahju
'1-balaghah* are worth reading.

In his old age, 'Ali had to make three more *jihads*

in the battles of Camel, Nahrawan and Siffin against the hypocrites, who rebelled and revolted against the commands of the Holy Qur'an and the Apostle of Allah.

Murder

Ali's effort to establish the Kingdom of Allah on earth, was cut short by the assassin's sword.

Ibn Muljam, the tool of Mu'awiyah, murdered 'Ali while he was saying his morning prayer and was crowned with martyrdom on 21st *Ramadan* 40 AH, and was buried in an-Najaf al-Ashraf (Iraq). (See photo on p.50)

Born in the House of Allah, the Ka'bah and was killed in the House of Allah, the Mosque of Kufah, the Lion of Allah, the most brave-hearted and gentle Muslim that ever lived, began his glorious life with devotion to Allah and His Apostle and ended it in the Service of Islam.

And do not speak of those who are slain in Allah's way as dead; nay (they are) *alive, but you do not perceive.* (2:154)

Chief of the Friends of Allah
(*Sayyid Awliya' Allah*)

Every God-fearing and pious Muslim knows `Ali, the Friend of Allah (*waliyyu 'llah*) In every place 'Ali is acknowledged as the Chief of the Friends of Allah. `Ali's benevolent powers are known and experienced even today, by those who love him and they will continue to be felt till the end of time.

`Ali, the Friend of Allah, does what pleases Allah and Allah grants what pleases Ali.

*   *   *

`Ali, the fierce and furious fighter of Khandaq, courageous and dauntless conqueror of Khaybar, was the
tender helper of the sick and the benefactor of widows
and orphans.

Ali, the Prince of charity-givers, working very hard
to earn money, overshadowed Hatim Ta'i, by giving away
a laden caravan to a beggar when he asked for a piece of
bread (for the sake of Allah).

Ali, who himself ate dry barley bread and salt,would
spread a banquet for the poor and the beggars.

Ali, the Ocean of knowledge, would not speak unless
asked.

In order to give dignity to honest labour, 'Ali rolled
up his sleeves and worked on the farms of Jews and
Muslims as a labourer.

The mighty Caliph of the Islamic Empire and Conqueror of eighty-three *jihads* would mend his, as well as
the Apostle's shoes.

There were many phrases of 'Ali and no man ever
knew him well.

The Holy Prophet of Islam said:

Nobody knows Allah except I and Ali.

Nobody knows me except Allah and Ali.

Nobody knows 'Ali except Allah and I.

If you want to see the knowledge of Adam, the piety
of Nuh, the devotion of Ibrahim, the awe of Musa and
the service and abstinence of `Isa look at the bright
face of `Ali.

'Ali said:

"The descendants of the Prophet are his confidants,
the shelter of his commands, the trustees of his knowledge, the stronghold of the Qur'an and the mountains
of his faith.

"It is they who have made the bent back of Islam straight. The Muslims were afraid of the unbelievers, but they made them bold and brave.

"None of the followers of Muhammad can be compared with the descendants of the Prophet. The recipients cannot be equal to the bestowers of blessings.

"The Ahlu 'l-bayt are the Foundation of Islam and the Pillars of Faith.

"Every Muslim is dependant upon them for help and guidance to attain salvation.

"They enjoy the privilege and right of Imamate and caliphate, which they retain. Now he who was the rightful and deserving heir to the caliphate has got it.

"The worshippers and followers of falsehood have always been in majority and the supporters of Truth have always been few in number.

"When the Prophet passed away, many people left the progeny of the Prophet and helped others. They left those whom they were ordered to love.

"The caliphate was handed over to other persons, who were worldly wise, with the usual human failings. They never had nor claimed any spiritual powers, nor were they sinless.

"O people! Let it be known to you that we are the descendants of the Holy Prophet. Angels come to us. We are the fountains of learning. We are the springs of wisdom and knowledge of Allah.

"He who is our friend and helper deserves the Mercy of Allah, and he who is our enemy, waits for the punishment of Allah. They speak lies against us and do injustice to us.

"Allah has elevated our position and he has made them inferior to us. He has opened the eyes of the people through us.

"Verily, the Imams shall be from Quraysh, who are the descendants of Banu Hashim. None but the Banu Hashim deserve Imamate.

"I advise you not to associate anything with Allah and do not spoil the *sunnah* of the Prophet. Keep these two pillars and you will be safe from blame and sins.

"Your religion is straight and your Imam wise. I was your friend during the lifetime of the Prophet. Know it well that the Imams are appointed caliphs by Allah. They rule over the people for Allah. Know it well that we are the true Companions of the Holy Prophet. We are the doors of his leamings. It is not lawful to enter houses, but through its doors. He who disregards this rule is a thief.

"Only those people who obey Allah and His Apostle shall go to Paradise and those who do otherwise shall go to Hell. Verily, Allah made you Muslims and He wants you to be sincere Muslims. He who recognizes Allah, His Prophet and his *Ahlu 'l-bayt* and even if he dies in bed and not in *jihad* he will be a martyr (*shahid*).

"O people! ask me (any question) before you miss me, because certainly I am acquainted with the passages of the sky more than the passages of the earth, and before that mischief springs upon its feet which would trample even the nose-string and destroy the wits of the people.

"Now, I bid you goodbye; you will find my place vacant and realize my worth. You will remember me when others succeed me to caliphate." (*Nahju 'l-baldghah*)

* * *

When Imam `Ali was fatally wounded by the poisoned sword of `Abdu 'r-Rahman ibn Muljam (the curse of Allah be on him), he (`Ali) made the following will to Imam

Hasan and Imam Husayn (peace be on them):

"I advise you (both) to fear Allah and that you should not hanker after the (pleasure of this) world even though it may run after you. Do not be sorry for anything of this world that you have been denied. Speak the truth and act (in expectation) for reward. Be an enemy of the oppressor and helper of the oppressed.

"I advise you (both) and all my children and members of my family and everyone whom my writing reaches, to fear Allah, to keep your affairs in order, and to maintain good relations among yourselves for I have heard your grandfather (the Holy Prophet) saying: `Improvement of mutual differences is better than general prayers and fastings.'

"(Fear) Allah (and) keep Allah in view in the matter of orphans. So do not allow them to starve and they should not be ruined in your presence.

"(Fear) Allah (and) keep Allah in view in the matter of your neighbours, because they were the subject of the Prophet's advice. He went on advising in their favour till we thought he would allow them a share in inheritance.

"(Fear) Allah (and) keep Allah in view in the matter of the Qur'an. No one should excel you in acting upon it.

"(Fear) Allah (and) keep Allah in view in the matter of prayer, because it is the pillar of your religion.

"(Fear) Allah (and) keep Allah in view in the matter of your Lord's House (Ka'bah). Do not forsake it so long as you live, because if it is abandoned you will not be spared.

"(Fear) Allah (and) keep Allah in view in the matter of *jihad* with the help of your property, lives and tongues in the way of Allah.

"You should keep to a respect for kinship and spending for others. Avoid turning away from one another and severing mutual relations. Do not give up bidding for good and forbidding from evil lest the mischievous gain positions over you, and then if you will pray, the prayers will not be granted."

MIHRAB (PRAYER NICHE) OF THE MOSQUE OF KUFAH
WHERE AMIR AL-MU'MININ 'ALI IBN ABI TALIB (A.S.)
WAS STRUCK WITH SWORD

THE FOURTH INFALLIBLE

THE SECOND IMAM

THE BURIAL PLACE OF IMAM HASAN IBN 'ALI (A.S.)
AT AL-BAQI', MEDINA.

AL-HASAN IBN ALI AL-MUJTABA
(Peace be on him)

Name: al-Hasan.
Title: al-Mujtaba.
Agnomen: Abu Muhammad.
Father's name: Ali Amir al-Mu'minin.
Mother's name: Fatimah (daughter of the Holy Prophet).
Birth: In Medina on Tuesday, 15th *Ramadan* 3 AH.
Death: Died at the age of 46, in Medina on Thursday, 28th *Safar* 50 AH; buried in Jannatu 'l-Baqi', in Medina.

IMAM HASAN was the eldest son of Imam `Ali and Hadrat Fatimah. When the Holy Prophet received the happy news of the birth of his grandson, he came to the house of his beloved daughter, took the newly born child in his arms, recited *adhan* and *iqamah* in his right and left ears respectively, and in compliance with Allah's command named him al-Hasan.

Childhood:
The first phase of seven years of his infancy was blessed with the gracious patronage of the Holy Prophet, who gifted him all his great qualities and adorned him

with Divine knowledge, tolerance, intelligence, bounty
and valour. Being infallible by birth and decorated with
heavenly knowledge by Allah, his insight had an access
to *al-lawhu 'l-mahfuz* (the Guarded Tablet on which
the transactions of mankind have been written by Allah
for all eternity).

The Holy Imam immediately became conversant with
all the contents of any *wahy* (Qur'anic verses) revealed
when the Holy Prophet would disclose it to his associates.
To the great surprise of the Holy Prophet, Hadrat Fatimah
would often recite the exact text of a newly revealed
wahy before he disclosed it personally to her. When he
inquired, she would inform him that it was Hasan through
whom she had learned the Revelation.

Remembrance of Allah:

The Holy Imam devoted himself to prayers in such
abundance, that all the limbs employed in prostration
bore scars and impressions of his *sajdah* (prostration).
Most of the nights were spent on the prayer-carpet. The
sense of his absorption and humiliation in prayers to
Allah were in such earnest that he would shed tears pro-
fusely out of fear of Allah. While performing ablution,
he trembled with the fear of Allah and his face grew pale
at the time of prayers. His earnest meditation in the offering of prayers and his extreme absorption in communion
with Allah would render him entirely unconscious of his
environments.

His Piousness and Contentment:

Imam Hasan had the worldly possessions at his disposal and could have well enjoyed a luxurious life, but
he utilized all of it in the betterment of the condition
of the poor.

He was so courteous and humble that he never hesitated to sit along with the beggars in the lanes and on the thoroughfares of Medina to reply to some of their religious queries. Through his cordial attitude and hospitality he never let the poor and the humble feel inferior to him when they visited his abode.

Imamate:

The demise of the Holy Prophet was followed by an eventful era when the Islamic world (under the false ruling bodies) came in the grip of the fever of expansionism and conquest. But even under such a revolutionary phase, Imam Hasan kept devoting himself to the sacred mission of peacefully propagating Islam and the teachings of the Holy Prophet along with his great father Imam 'Ali.

The martyrdom of Imam Ali on the 21st *Ramadan* marked the inception of Imam Hasan's Imamate. The majority of Muslims pledged their allegiance to him and finalized the formality of *bay'ah* (oath of allegiance). No sooner had he taken the reins of leadership into his hands than he had to meet the challenge of Mu'awiyah, the Governor of Syria, who declared a war against him. In compliance with the Will of Allah and with a view to refrain from causing the massacre of Muslims however, he entered into a piece treaty with Mu'awiyah on terms (though not totally respected and carried out by Mu'awiyah), yet saved Islam and stopped a civil war. But this peace treaty was never meant as a surrender by him of the permanent leadership to Mu'awiyah. It was meant only as an interim transfer of the administration of the Islamic kingdom, subject to the condition that the administration would be surrendered bact to Imam Hasan after Mu'awiyah's death and then it would in turn be inherited by Imam Husayn. Having relieved himself of the administrative responsibilities, Imam Hasan kept the religious leadership with himself and devoted his life to the propagation of Islam and the teachings of the Holy Prophet in Medina.

Martyrdom:

Mu'dwiyah's malice against Imam Hasan led him to conspire with the Imam's wife Ja'dah, the daughter of Ash'ath. She was made to give the Imam some poison which affected his liver. Imam Hasan thus succumbed to Mu'dwiyah's fatal mischief and attained his martyrdom on 28th Safar 50 AH. His funeral was attended by Imam Husayn and the members of the Hashimite family. His bier while being taken for burial to the Holy Prophet's tomb was shot at with arrows by his enemies, (under direct supervision and consent of A'ishah), and it had to be diverted for burial to the Jannatu'l-Bagi` at Medina. His tomb was demolished along with others on 8th Shawwdl 1344 (21st April 1926) by the Saudi rulers when they came to power in Hijaz.

The terms of the peace treaty were soon violated, but earned only a short-lived glory for Mu'dwiyah. Its aftermath proved disastrous and doomed the fate of his son Yazid and dealt a fatal blow to the entire family of Umayyads. After the death of Mu'awiyah, Imam Husayn emerged as the insurmountable mountain of truth and determination. In the gruesome tragedy of Karbala', by sheer force of numbers, and by isolating the seventy-two members of Imam Husayn's party and stopping them from even getting water to drink for three days, Yazid succeeded in annihilating the seventy-two persons including members of the Imam's family who were with him.

This dastardly success of Yazid was, however, short-lived. The Muslims turned against him on learning of the heinous act he had committed and this resulted in the downfall of Yazid and the extinction of the Umayyad power from the face of the earth.

al-`Allamah at-Tabataba'i writes:

Imam Hasan Mujtaba, upon whom be peace, was the second Imam. He and his brother Imam Husayn were the two sons of Amir al-Mu'minin `Ali and Hadrat Fatimah, the daughter of the Prophet. Many times the Prophet had said, "Hasan and Husayn are my children." Because of these same words `Ali would say to his other children, "You are my children and Hasan and Husayn are the children of the Prophet."

Imam Hasan was born in the year 3 AH, in Medina and shared in the life of the Prophet for somewhat over seven years, growing up during that time under his loving care. After the death of the Prophet which was no more than three, or according to some, six months earlier than the death of Hadrat Fatimah, Hasan was placed directly under the care of his noble father. After the death of his father, through Divine Command and according to the will of his father, Imam Hasan became Imam; he also occupied the outward function of caliph for about six months, during which time he administered the affairs of the Muslims. During that time Mu'5wiyah, who was a bitter enemy of `Ali and his family and had fought for years with the ambition of capturing the caliphate, first on the pretext of avenging the death of the third caliph and finally with an open claim to the caliphate, marched his army to Iraq, the seat of Imam Hasan's caliphate. War ensued during which Mu'awiyah gradually subverted the generals and commanders of Imam Hasan's army with large sums of money and deceiving promises until the army rebelled against Imam Hasan. Finally, the Imam was forced to make peace and to yield the caliphate to Mu'awiyah, provided it would again return to Imam Hasan after Mu'awiyah's death and the Im5m's Household and partisans would be protected in every way.

In this way Mu'awiyah captured the Islamic caliphate and entered Iraq. In a public speech he officially made null and void all the peace conditions and in every way possible placed the severest pressure upon the members of the Household of the Prophet and the Shi'ah. During all the ten years of his Imamate, Imam Hasan lived in conditions of extreme hardship and under persecution, with no security even in his own house. In the year 50 AH, he was poisoned and martyred by one of his own House-hold who, as has been accounted by historians, had been motivated by Mu'awiyah.

In human perfection Imam Hasan was reminiscent of his father and a perfect example of his noble grand-father. In fact, as long as the Prophet was alive, he and his brother were always in the company of the Prophet who even sometimes would carry them on his shoulders. Both Sunni and Shi`ite sources have transmitted this saying of the Holy Prophet concerning Hasan and Husayn: "These two children of mine are Imams (leaders) whether they stand up or sit down" (allusion to whether they occupy the external function of caliphate or not). Also, there are many traditions of the Holy Prophet and `Ali concerning the fact that Imam Hasan would gain the func-tion of Imamate after his noble father. (Shi`ite Islam)

قال الإمام الحَسَنُ بن عليّ عليهما السَّلام :

• اجْعَلْ مَا طَلَبْتَ مِنَ آلدُّنْيَا فَلَمْ تَظْفَرْ بِهِ بِمَنْزِلَةِ مَا لَمْ يَخْطُرْ بِبَالِكَ.

• مَا تَشَاوَرَ قَوْمٌ إِلاَّ هُدُوا إِلَى رُشْدِهِمْ.

• الْقَرِيبُ مَنْ قَرَّبَتْهُ الْمَوَدَّةُ وَ إِنْ بَعُدَ نَسَبُهُ، وَالْبَعِيدُ مَنْ بَاعَدَتْهُ الْمَوَدَّةُ وَ إِنْ قَرُبَ نَسَبُهُ.

• الْفُرصَةُ سَرِيعَةُ الْفَوْتِ بَعِيدَةُ الْعَوْدِ.

al-Imam al-Hasan ibn Ali, peace be on him, said:

* If you fail to obtain something of worldly benefit, take it as if the thought of it had never crossed your mind at all.

* Never did a nation resort to mutual counsel except that they were guided by it towards maturity.

* It is love which brings closer those who are remote by ancestry, and it is (the absence of) love which causes dissociation between those who are related by ancestry.

* Opportunity is something which is quick to vanish and late to return.

* * * * *

THE FIFTH INFALLIBLE

THE THIRD IMAM

THE HOLY SHRINE OF IMAM HUSAYN (A.S.)
AT KARBALA' (IRAQ).

AL-HUSAYN IBN ALI SAYYIDU'SH-SHUHADA'
(Peace be on him)

Name: **al-Husayn**
Title: Sayyidu 'sh-Shuhada'.
Agnomen: Abu `Abdillah.
Father's name: Ali Amir al-Mu'minin.
Mother's name: Fatimah (daughter of the Holy Prophet).
Birth: In Medina on Thursday, 3rd *Sha'ban* 4 AH.
Death: Martyred in Karbala' (Iraq) at the age of 57, on
Friday, 10th *Muharram* 61 AH and buried there.

IN THE house of the Holy Prophet, which presented the
best image of both the worlds - the heaven and the earth
- a child who benefited humanity as if he was a Divine
Impression reflecting the earth, was born on one of the
nights of the month of *Sha`ban.* His father was Imam Ali,
the best model of kindness towards his friends and the
bravest against the enemies of Islam, and his mother was
Hadrat Fatimah, the only daughter and child of the Holy
Prophet, who had as univesally acknowledged, inherited
the qualities of her father.

Imam Husayn, is the third Apostolic Imam. When
the good news of his birth reached the Holy Prophet, he

came to his daughter's house, took the newly-born child in his arms, recited *adhan* and *iqamah* in his right and left ears respectively, and on the 7th day of his birth, after performing the rites of *aqiqah*, named him al-Husayn, in compliance with Allah's command.

'Abdullah ibn Abbas relates: "On the very day when Imam Husayn was born, Allah ordered angel Gabriel to descend and congratulate the Holy Prophet on His Behalf and on his own. While descending, Gabriel passed over an island where the angel Futrus had been banished due to his delay in executing a commission assigned by Allah. He was deprived of his wings and expelled to the island where he remained for several years praying and worshipping Allah and asking for His forgiveness.

"When the angel Futrus saw Gabriel, he called out, 'Where are you going, O Gabriel?' To this he replied, 'Husayn, the grandson of Muhammad is born, and for this very reason Allah has commanded me to convey His congratulations to His Apostle.' Thereupon, the angel said, ` Can you carry me also along with you? May Muhammad recommend my case to Allah.' Gabriel took the angel along with him, came to the Holy Prophet, offered congratulations to him on behalf of Allah and himself and referred the case of the angel to him. The Holy Prophet said to Gabriel, `Ask the angel to touch the body of the newly-born child and return to his place in Heaven.' On doing this, the angle re-obtained his wings instantly and praising the Holy Prophet and his newly-born grandson, ascended towards the Heaven."

Hasan and Husayn, the two sons of the Holy Imam Ali ibn Abi Talib and Hadrat Fatimah, our Lady of Light, were respected and revered as the `Leaders of the Youths of Paradise' as stated by the Holy Prophet.

The Holy Prophet Muhammad, peace be on him and

his progeny, had openly prophesied that the faith of Islam would be rescued by his second grandson Husayn, when Yazid, son of Mu'awiayh, would endeavour to destroy it.

Yazid was known for his devilish character and brutish conduct. He was known as the most licentious of men. The people having known and understood the character of Yazid, formed a covenant by which Mu'awiyah could not appoint Yazid as his successor. This undertaking was given by Mu'awiyah to Imam Hasan from whom Mu'awiyah had snatched power. Mu'awiyah violated this undertaking and nominated Yazid who succeded his father.

Immediately as he came to power, Yazid began acting in full accordance with his known character. He started interfering in the fundamentals of the faith and ,practised every vice and wickedness freely with the highest degree of impunity and yet held himself out as the successor of the Holy Prophet, demanding allegiance to himself as the leading guide of the faith. Paying allegiance to Yazid was nothing short of acknowledging the devil as God. If a divine personality like the Holy Imam Husayn had agreed to his authority, it would be actually recommending the devil to humanity in place of God. Yazid demanded allegiance from the Holy Imam Husayn, who could have never agreed to it at any cost. The people fearing death and destruction at the hands of the tyrant had yielded to him out of fear. Imam Husayn said that come whatever may, he would never yield to the devil in place of God and undo what his grandfather, the Holy Prophet had established.

The refusal of the Holy Imam to pay allegiance to this fiend, marked the start of the persecution of the Holy Imam. As a result he had retired to Medina where he led a secluded life. Even here he was not allowed to live in peace, and was forced to seek refuge in Mecca -

where also he was badly harassed, and Yazid plotted to murder him in the very precincts of the great sanctuary of Ka'bah.

In order to safeguard the great sanctuary, Imam Husayn decided to leave Mecca for Kufah just a day before the *hajj* pilgrimage. When asked the reason for the mysterious departure from Mecca foregoing the pilgrimage which was only the next day, Imam Husayn said that he would perform this year's pilgrimage at Karbala', offering the sacrifice not of any animals, but of his kith and kin and some faithful friends. He enumerated the names of his kith and kin who would lay down their lives with him in the great sacrifice at Karbala'.

The people of Kufah getting tired of the tyrannic and satanic rule of Yazid, had written innumerable letters and sent emissaries to Imam Husayn to come over and give them guidance in faith. Although Imam Husayn knew the ultimate end of the invitations, he as the divinely chosen Imam could not refuse to give the guidance sought for. When the Holy Imam with his entourage had reached Karbala', his horse mysteriously stopped and would not move any further. Upon this the Holy Imam declared: "This is the land, the land of sufferings and tortures." He alighted from his horse, and ordered his followers to encamp there saying: "Here shall we be martyred and our children be killed. Here shall our tents be burned and our family arrested. This is the land about which my grandfather the Holy Prophet had foretold, and his prophecy will certainly be fulfilled."

On the 7th of *Muharram* water supply to the Imam's camp was cut and the torture of thirst and hunger started. The Holy Imam's camp consisted of ladies, innocent child ren including babies and some male members of the Holy Prophet's family; along with a small band of some faithful friends of Imam Husayn who had chosen to die with the Holy Imam, fighting against the devil for the cause of Allah.

The Day of `Ashura (10th of *Muharram*):

At dawn the Imam glanced over the army of Yazid and saw `Umar ibn Sa'd ordering his forces to march towards him. He gathered his followers and addressed them thus: "Allah has, this day, permitted us to be engaged in a Holy War and He shall reward us for our martyrdom. So prepare yourselves to fight against the enemies of Islam with patience and resistance. O sons of the noble and self-respecting persons, be patient! Death is nothing but a bridge which you must cross after facing trials and tribulations so as to reach Heaven and its joys. Which of you do not like to go from this prison (world) to the lofty palaces (Paradise)?"

Having heard the Imam's address, all his companions were overwhelmed and cried out, "O our Master! We are all ready to defend you and your Ahlu 'l-bayt, and to sacrifice our lives for the cause of Islam."

Imam Husayn sent out from his camp one after another to fight and sacrifice their lives in the way of the Lord. Lastly, when all his men and children had laid down their lives, Imam Husayn brought his six-month old baby son `Ali al-Asghar, and offering him on his own hands, demanded some water for the baby, dying of thirst. The thirst of the baby was quenched by a deadly poisoned arrow from the brute's forces, which pinned the baby's neck to the arm of the helpless father. At last when the six-month old baby also was killed, Imam Husayn addressed Allah: "O Lord! Thy Husayn has offered in Thy way whatever Thou hath blessed him with. Bless Thy Husayn, 0 Lord! with the acceptance of this sacrifice.

Everything Husayn could do till now was through Thy help and by Thy Grace." Lastly, Imam Husayn came into the field and was killed, the datails of which merciless slaughter are heart rending. The forces of Yazid having killed Imam Husayn, cut and severed his head from his body and raised it on a lance. The severed head of the Holy Imam began glorifying Allah from the point of the lance saying, '*A llahu A kbar'*. "All glory be to Allah Who is the Greatest!"

After the wholesale, merciless and most brutal slaughter of the Holy Imam with his faithful band, the helpless ladies and children along with the ailing son of Imam Husayn, Imam `Ali Zaynu '1-`Abidin, were taken captives.

Some Sayings of the Holy Prophet During his Lifetime with Reference to Imam Husayn:

1. Hasan and Husayn are the Leaders of the Youths of Paradise.

2. Husayn is from me and I am from Husayn, Allah befriends those who befriend Husayn and He is the enemy of those who bear enmity to him.

3. Whosoever wishes to see such a person who lives on earth but whose dignity is honoured by the Heaven-dwellers, should see my grandson Husayn.

4. O my son! thy flesh is my flesh and thy blood is my blood; thou art a leader, the son of a leader and the brother of a leader; thou art a spiritual guide, the son of a spiritual guide and the brother of a spiritual guide; thou art an Apostolical Imam, the son of an Apostolical Imam and the brother of an Apostolical Imam; thou art the father of nine Imams, the ninth of whom would be the Qa'im (the last infallible spiritual guide).

5. The punishment inflicted on the murderer of Husayn in Hell would be equal to half of the total punish-

ment to be imposed on the entire sinners of the world.

6. When the Holy Prophet informed Hadrat Fatimah of the martyrdom in store for his grandson, she burst into tears and asked, "O my father! when would my son be martyred?" "In such a critical moment," replied the Holy Prophet, "When neither I nor you, nor `Ali would be alive." This accentuated her grief and she inquired again, "Who then, O my father, would commemorate Husayn's martyrdom?" The Holy Prophet said, "The men and the women of a particular sect of my followers, who will befriend my Ahlu 'l-bayt, will mourn for Husayn and commemorate his martyrdom each year in every century."

Ibn Sa'd narrates from ash-Sha'bi:

Imam Ali, while on his way to Siffin, passed through the desert of Karbala', there he stopped and wept very bitterly. When interrogated regarding the cause of his weeping, he commented that one day he visited the Holy Prophet and found him weeping. When he asked the Apostle of Allah as to what was the reason which made him weep, he replied, "O Ali, Gabriel has just been with me and informed me that my son Husayn would be martyred in Karbala', a place near the bank of the River Euphrates. This moved me so much that I could not help weeping."

Anas ibn Harith narrates:

One day the Holy Prophet ascended the pulpit to deliver a sermon to his associates while Imam Husayn and Imam Hasan were sitting before him. When his address was over, he put his left hand on Imam Husayn and raising his head towards Heaven, said: "O my Lord! I am Muhammad Thy slave and Thy Prophet, and these two are the distin-

guished and pious members of my family who would
fortify my cause after me. O my Lord! Gabriel has informed me that my son Husayn would be killed. O my
Lord! bless my cause in recompense for Husayn's martyrdom, make him the leader of the martyrs, be Thou his
helper and guardian and do not bless his murderers."

Sir Muhammad Iqbal says:

Imam Husayn uprooted despotism forever till the
Day of Resurrection. He watered the dry garden of freedom with the surging wave of his blood, and indeed he
awakened the sleeping Muslim nation.

If Imam Husayn had aimed at acquiring a worldly
empire, he would not have travelled the way he did (from
Medina to Karbala'). Husayn weltered in blood and dust
for the sake of truth. Verily he, therefore, became the
bed-rock (foundation) of the Muslim creed; *la ilaha illa
Allah* (There is no god but Allah).

Khwaja Mu'inu 'd-Din Chishti says:

He gave his head, but did not put his hand into the
hands of Yazid. Verily, Husayn is the foundation of *la
ilaha illa Allah.* Husayn is lord and the lord of lords.

Husayn himself is Islam and the shield of Islam.
Though he gave his head (for Islam) but never pledged
Yazid. Truly Husayn is the founder of "There is no Deity
except Allah."

Brown in his A Literary History of Persia writes:

As a reminder, the blood-stained field of Karbala'
where the grandson of the Apostle of-God fell at length,
tortured by thirst and surrounded by the bodies of his
murdered kinsmen, has been at any time since then suffi-
cient to evoke, even in the most lukewarm and heedless,

the deepest emotion, the most frantic grief and the exaltation of spirit before which pain, danger, and death shrink to unconsidered trifles. Yearly, on the tenth day of *Muharram,* the tragedy is rehearsed in Persia, in India, in Turkey, in Egypt, wherever a Shi 'ite community or colony exists; . . . As I write it all comes back; the wailing chant, the sobbing multitudes, the white raiment red with blood from self-inflicted wounds, the intoxication of grief and sympathy.

al-Allamah at-Tabataba'i writes:

Imam Husayn (Sayyidu'sh-Shuhada', "the lord among martyrs"), the second child of 'Ali and Fatimah, was born in the year 4 AH, and after the martyrdom of his brother, Imam Hasan Mujtaba, became Imam through Divine Command and his brother's will. Imam Husayn was Imam for a period of ten years, all but the last six months coinciding with the caliphate of Mu'awiyah. Imam Husayn lived under the most difficult outward conditions of suppression and persecution. This was due to the fact that, first of all, religious laws and regulations had lost much of their weight and credit, and the edicts of the Umayyad government had gained complete authority and power. Secondly, Mu'awiyah and his aides made use of every possible means to put aside and move out of the way the Household of the Prophet and the Shi'ah, and thus obliterate the name of Ali and his family. And above all, Mu'awiyah wanted to strengthen the basis of the caliphate of his son, Yazid, who because of his lack of principles and scruples was opposed by a large group of Muslims. Therefore, in order to quell all opposition, Mu'awiyah had undertaken newer and more severe measures. By force and necessity Imam Husayn had to endure these days and to tolerate every kind of mental and spiritual agony and affliction from

Mu'awiyah and his aides - until in the middle of the year 60 AH, Mu'awiyah died and his son Yazid took his place.

Paying allegiance (*bay'ah*) was an old Arab practice which was carried out in important matters such as that of kingship and governorship. Those who were ruled, and especially the well-known among them, would give their hand in allegiance, agreement and obedience to their king or prince and in this way would show their support for his actions. Disagreement after allegiance was considered as disgrace and dishonour for a people and, like breaking an agreement after having signed it officially, it was considered as a definite crime. Following the example of the Holy Prophet, people believed that allegiance, when given by free will and not through force, carried authority and weight.

Mu'awiyah had asked the well-known among the people to give their allegiance to Yazid, but had not imposed this request upon Imam Husayn. He had especially told Yazid in his last will that if Husayn refused to pay allegiance he should pass over it in silence and overlook the matter, for he had understood correctly the disastrous consequences which would follow if the issue were to be pressed. But because of his egoism and recklessness, Yazid neglected his father's advice and immediately after the death of his father ordered the governor of Medina either to force a pledge of allegiance from Imam Husayn or send his head to Damascus.

After the governor of Medina informed Imam Husayn of this demand, the Imam, in order to think over the question, asked for a delay and overnight started with his family toward Mecca. He sought refuge in the sanctuary of God which in Islam is the official place of refuge and security. This event occurred toward the end of the month of *Rajab* and the beginning of *Sha'ban* of 60 AH.

For nearly four months Imam Husayn stayed in Mecca in refuge. This news spread throughout the Islamic world. On the one hand many people who were tired of the iniquities of Mu'awiyah's rule and were even more dissatisfied when Yazid became caliph, corresponded with Imam Husayn and expressed their sympathy for him. On the other hand, a flood of letters began to flow, especially from Iraq and particularly the city of Kufah, inviting the Imam to go to Iraq and accept the leadership of the populace there with the aim of beginning an uprising to overcome injustice and iniquity. Naturally, such a situation was dangerous for Yazid.

The stay of Imam Husayn in Mecca continued until the season for pilgrimage when Muslims from all over the world poured in groups into Mecca in order to perform the rites of the *hajj*. The Imam discovered that some of the followers of Yazid had entered Mecca as pilgrims (*hajjis*) with the mission to kill the Imam during the rites of *hajj* with the arms they carried under their special pilgrimage dress (*ihram*).

The Imam shortened the pilgrimage rites and decided to leave. Amidst the vast crowd of people he stood up in a short speech announced that he was setting out for Iraq. In this short speech he also declared that he would be martyred and asked Muslims to help him in attaining the goal he had in view and to offer their lives in the path of God. On the next day he set out with his family and a group of his comapanions for Iraq.

Imam Husayn was determined not to give his allegiance to Yazid and knew full well that he would be killed. He was aware that his death was inevitable in the face of the awesome military power of the Umayyads, supported as it was by corruption in certain sectors, spiritual decline, and lack of will power among the people, especially in Iraq.

Some of the outstanding people of Mecca stood in the way of Imam Husayn and warned him of the danger of the move he was making. But he answered that he refused to pay allegiance and give his approval to a government of injustice and tyranny. He added that he knew that wherever he turned or went he would be killed. He would leave Mecca in order to preserve the respect for the House of God and not allow this respect to be destroyed by having his blood spilled there.

While on the way to Kufah and still a few days journey away from the city, he received news that the agent of Yazid in Kufah had put to death the representative of the Imam in that city and also one of the Imam's determined supporters who was a well-known man in Kufah. Their feet had been tied and they had been dragged through the streets. The city and its surroundings were placed under strict observation and countless soldiers of the enemy were awaiting him. There was no way open to him but to march ahead and to face death. It was here that the Imam expressed his definitive determination to go ahead and be martyred; and so he continued on his journey.

Approximately seventy kilometres from Kufah in a desert named Karbala', the Imam and his entourage were surrounded by the army of Yazid. For eight days they stayed in this spot during which the circle narrowed and the number of the enemy's army increased. Finally the Imam, with his Household and a small number of companions were encircled by an army of thirty thousand soldiers. During these days the Imam fortified his position and made a final selection of his companions. At night he called his companions and during a short speech stated that there was nothing ahead but death and martyrdom. He added that since the enemy was concerned only with his person he would free them from all obligations so that anyone who wished could escape in the darkness of the night and save his life. Then he ordered the lights to be turned out and most of his companions, who had joined him for their own advantage, dispersed. Only a handful of those who loved the truth about forty of his close aides and some of the Banu Hashim remained.

Once again the Imam assembled those who were left and put them to a test. He addressed his companions and Hashimite relatives, saying again that the enemy was concerned only with his person. Each could benefit from the darkness of the night and escape the danger. But this time the faithful companions of the Imam answered each in his own way that they would not deviate for a moment from the path of truth of which the Imam was the leader and would never leave him alone. They said they would defend his Household to the last drop of their blood and as long as they could carry a sword.

On the ninth day of the month the last challenge to choose between "allegiance or war" was made by the enemy to the Imam. The Imam asked for a delay in order to worship overnight and became determined to enter battle on the next day.

On the tenth day of *Muharram* of the year 61 (680) the Imam lined up before the enemy with his small band of followers, less than ninety persons consisting of forty of his companions, thirty some members of the army of the enemy that joined him during the night and day of war, and his Hashimite family of children, brothers, nephews, nieces and cousins. That day they fought from morning until their final breath, and the Imam, the young Hashimites and the companions were all martyred. Among those killed were two children of Imam Hasan, who were only thirteen and eleven years old; and a five-year-old child and a suckling baby of Imam Husayn.

The army of the enemy, after ending the war, plundered the *haram* of the Imam and burned his tents. They decapitated the bodies of the martyrs, denuded them and threw them to the ground without burial. Then they moved the members of the *haram*, all of whom were helpless women and girls, along with the heads of the martyrs, to Kufah. Among the prisoners there were three male members: a twenty-two years old son of Imam Husayn who was very ill and unable to move, namely, `Ali ibn al-Husayn, the fourth Imam; his four years old son, Muhammad ibn Ali, who became the fifth Imam; and finally Hasan al-Muthanna, the son of the second Imam who was also the son-in-law of Imam Husayn and who, having been wounded during the war, lay among the dead. They found him near death and through the intercession of one of the generals did not cut off his head. Rather, they took him with the prisoners to Kufah and from there to Damascus before Yazid.

The event of Karbala', the capture of the women and children of the Household of the Prophet, their being taken as prisoners from town to town and the speeches made by the daughter of `Ali, Zaynab, and the fourth Imam who were among the prisoners, disgraced the Umayyads. Such abuse of the Household of the Prophet annulled the propaganda which Mu'awiyah had carried out for years. The matter reached such proportions that Yazid in public disowned and condemned the actions of his agents. The event of Karbala' was a major factor in the overthrow of Umayyad's rule although its effect was delayed. It also strengthened the roots of Shi'ism. Among its immediate results were the revolts and rebellions combined with bloody wars which continued for twelve years. Among those who were instrumental in the death of the Imam not one was able to escape revenge and punishment.

Anyone who studies closely the history of the life of Imam Husayn and Yazid and the conditions that prevailed at that time, and analyses this chapter of Islamic history, will have no doubt that in those circumstances there was no choice before Imam Husayn but to be killed. Swearing allegiance to Yazid would have meant publicly showing contempt for Islam, something which was not possible for the Imam, for Yazid not only showed no respect for Islam and its injunction but also made a public demonstration of impudently treading under foot its basis and its laws. Those before him, even if they opposed religious injunctions, always did so in the guise of religion, and at least formally respected religion. They took pride in being companions of the Holy Prophet and the other religious figures in whom people believed. From this it can be concluded that the claim of some interpreters of these events is false when they say that the two brothers, Hasan and Husayn, had two different tastes and that one chose the way of peace and the other the way of war, so that one brother made peace with Mu'awiyah although he had an army of forty thousand while the other went to war against Yazid with an army of forty. For we see that this same Imam Husayn, who refused to pay allegiance to Yazid for one day, lived for ten years under the rule of Mu'awiyah, in the same manner as his brother who also had endured for ten years under Mu'awiyah, without opposing him.

It must be said in truth that if Imam Hasan or Imam Husayn had fought Mu'awiyah they would have been killed without there being the least benefit for Islam. Their deaths would have had no effect before the righteous appearing policy of Mu'awiyah, a competent politician who emphasized his being a companion of the Holy Prophet, the "scribe of the revelation," and "uncle of the faithful" and who used every stratagem possible to preserve a religious guise for his rule. Moreover, with his ability to set the stage to accomplish his desires he could have had them killed by their own people and then assumed a state of mourning and sought to revenge their blood, just as he sought to give the impression that he was avenging the killing of the third caliph. (Shi`ite Islam)

قال الإمام الحُسين بن علي عليهما السَّلام .

«إِيَّاكَ وَ مَا تَعْتَذِرُ مِنْهُ (تجنَّب ما تعتذر منه)، فَإِنَّ المُؤْمِنَ لاَ يُسِئُ وَلاَ يَعْتَذِرُ، وَالمُنَافِقُ كُلَّ يَوم يُسِئُ وَ يَعْتَذِرُ.

«اعْلَمُوا إِنَّ جَوائِجَ النَّاسِ إِلَيْكُمْ مِنْ نِعَمِ أَللهِ عَلَيْكُمْ فَلاَ تَمَلُّوا النَّعَمَ فَتَتَحَوَّلَ إِلَى غَيْرِكُمْ .

«إِنَّ أَلنَّاسَ عَبِيدُ أَلدُّنَيا وَأَلدّينُ لَعْقُ عَلَى أَلسِنَتِهِمْ يَحُوطُونَهُ مَا دَرَّتْ مَعَايِشُهُمْ فَإِذَا مُحِّصُوا بِالبَلاءِ قَلَّ أَلدَّيَّانُونَ .

«طُولُ التَّجَارِبِ زِيَادَةٌ فِي الْعَقِلِ .

al-Imam al-Husayn ibn `Ali, peace be on him, said:

  * Beware of your apologies; for a true believer does not sin and does not have to apologize, whereas the hypocrite commits sins everyday and apologizes everyday.

  * When other people turn to you in need, consider it a favour of Allah. Do not be wearied of this favour, or it will move on to someone else.

  * Experience enhances the intellect.

*   *   *   *   *

THE SIXTH INFALLIBLE

THE FOURTH IMAM

THE BURIAL PLACE OF IMAM `ALI IBN HUSAYN
ZAYNU 'L-`ABIDIN (A.S.) AT AL-BAQI',MEDINA.

ALI IBN AL-HUSAYN ZAYNU'L-`ABIDIN
(Peace be on him)

Name: **Ali**.
Title: Zaynu 'l-`Abidin.
Agnomen: Abu Muhammad.
Father's name: al-Husayn Sayyidu 'sh-Shuhada'.
Mother's name: Shahr Banu, daughter of Yazdeger III,
    the King of Persia.
Birth: In Medina, on Saturday, 15th *Jumadi 'l-ula* 36 AH.
Death: Died at the age of 58, in Medina; poisoned by
    al-Walid ibn `Abdi'l-Malik ibn Marwan on 25th *Muhar-
    ram* 95 AH; buried in Jannatu 'l-Baqi', in Medina..

THE HOLY Imam `Ali Zaynu 'l-Abidin is the Fourth Apos-
tolic Imam. His epithet was Abu Muhammad and was
popularly titled as "Zaynu 'l-Abidin". The mother of
this Holy Imam was the royal personage, Shahr Banu, the
daughter of King Yazdegerd, the last pre-Islamic Ruler
of Persia.

Imam Zaynu 'l-`Abidin spent the first two years of
his infancy in the lap of his grandfather `Ali ibn Abi Talib
and then for twelve years he had the gracious patronage
of his uncle, the second Holy Imam al-Hasan ibn `Ali. In

109

61 AH, he was present in Karbala', at the time of the gruesome tragedy of the wholesale massacre of his father, his uncles, his brothers, his cousins and all the godly comrades of his father; and suffered a heartless captivity and imprisonment at the hands of the devilish forces of Yazid.

When Imam Husayn had come for the last time to his camp to bid goodbye to his family, `Ali Zaynu 'l-`Abidin was lying semi- conscious in his sickbed and hence he escaped the massacre in Karbala'. Imam Husayn could only manage a very brief talk with the inmates of his camp and departed nominating his sick son as Imam.

The Holy Imam Zaynu 'l- Abidin lived for about thirty-four years after his father and all his life he passed in prayers and supplication to Allah and in remembrance of his martyred father. It is for his ever being in prayers to Allah, mostly lying in prayerful prostration, that this Holy Imam was popularly called "Sajjad".

The knowledge and piety of this Holy Imam was matchless. az-Zuhri, al-Waqidi and Ibn `Uyaynah say that they could not find any one equal to him in piety and godliness. He was so mindful of Allah that whenever he sat for ablution for prayers, the complexion of his face would change and when he stood at prayer his body was seen trembling. When asked why this was, he replied, "Know ye not before whom I stand in prayer, and with whom I hold discourse?"

Even on the gruesome day of Ashura when Yazid's forces had massacred his father, his kith and kin and his comrades and had set fire to the camp, this Holy Imam was engrossed in his supplications to the Lord.

When the brutal forces of Yazid's army had taken the ladies and children as captives, carrying them seated on the bare back of the camels, tied in ropes; this Holy Imam, though sick, was put in heavy chains with iron rings round his neck and his ankles, and was made to walk barefooted on the thorny plains from Karbala' to Kufah and to Damascus; and even then this godly soul never was unmindful of his prayers to the Lord and was always thankful and supplicative to Him.

His charity was unassuming and hidden. After his passing away, the people said that hidden charity ended with the departure of this Holy Imam. Like his grand father Ali ibn Abi Talib, Ali Zaynu 'l-Abidin used to carry on his own back at night bags of flour and bread for the poor and needy families in Medina and he so maintained hundred of poor families in the city.

The Holy Imam was not only hospitable even to his enemies but also used to continually exhort them to the right path.

Imam Zaynu 'l-`Abidin along with the *Ahlu 'l-bayt* passed through dreadful and very dangerous times, for the aggressions and atrocities of the tyrant rulers of the age had reached a climax. There was plunder, pillage, and murder everywhere. The teachings of Islam were observed more in their breach. The heartless tyrant al-Hajjaj ibn Yusuf ath Thagafi was threatening every one who professed allegiance or devotion to the *Ahlu 'l--bayt;* and those caught were mercilessly put to death. The movement of the Holy Imam was strictly restricted and his meeting with any person was totally banned. Spies were employed to trace out the adherents of the *Ahlu 'l-bayt.* Practically every house was searched and every family scrutinized.

Imam Zaynu 'l-Abidin was not given the time to offer his prayers peacefully, nor could he deliver any sermons. This God's Vicegerent on earth therefore, adopted a third course which proved to be very beneficial to his followers. This was in compiling supplicative prayers for the daily use of man in his endeavour to approach the Almighty Lord.

The invaluable collection of his edited prayers are known as *as-Sahifah al-Kamilah* or *as-Sahifah as-Sajjddiyyah;* it is known also *as az-Zabur* (Psalm) of *A al Muhammad.* The collection is an invaluable treasury of wonderfully effective supplications to the Lord in inimitably beautiful language. Only those who have ever come across those supplications would know the excellence and the beneficial effect of these prayers. Through these prayers the Imam gave all the necessary guidance to the faithful during his seclusion.

On the 25th of *Muharram* 95 AH when he was in Medina, al-Walid ibn Abdi 'l-Malik ibn Marwan, the then ruler got this Holy Imam martyred by poison. The funeral prayers for this Holy Imam were conducted by his son the Fifth Imam, Muhammad al-Baqir and his body was laid to rest in the cemetery of Jannatu '1-Bagi ' in Medina.

al-`Allamah at-Tabataba'i writes:

Imam Sajjad (Ali ibn al-Husayn entitled Zaynu 'l-Abidin and Sajjad) was the son of the Third Imam and his wife, the queen among women, the daughter of Yaz degerd the King of Iran. He was the only son of Imam Husayn to survive, for his other three brothers `Ali Akbar, aged twenty-five, five-year-old Ja'far and `Ali al-Asghar (or Abdullah) who was a suckling baby were martyred during the event of Karbala'. The Imam had also accompanied his father on the journey that terminated fatally in Karbala', but because of severe illness and the inability to carry arms or participate in fighting he was prevented from taking part in the holy war and being martyred. So he was sent with the womenfolk to Damascus. After spending a period in imprisonment he was sent with honour to Medina because Yazid wanted to conciliate public opinion. But for a second time, by the order of

the Umayyad caliph, `Abdu 'l-Malik, he was chained and
sent from Medina to Damascus and then again returned
to Medina.

The Fourth Imam, upon returning to Medina, retired
from public life completely, closed the door of his house
to strangers and spent his time in worship. He was in contact only with the elite among the Shiites such as Abu
Hamzah ath-Thumali, Abu Khalid Kabuli and the like.
The elite disseminated among the Shi'ah the religious
sciences they learned from the Imam. In this way Shi'ism
spread considerably and showed its effects during the
Imamate of the Fifth Imam. Among the works of the
Fourth Imam is a book called *Sahifah Sajjadiyyah.* It con-
sists of fifty-seven prayers concerning the most sublime
Divine sciences and is known as "The Psalm of the Household of the Prophet."

The Fourth Imam died (according to some Shiite
traditions poisoned by al-Walid ibn `Abdi 'l-Malik ibn
Marwan through the instigation of the Umayyad caliph
Hisham) in 95/712 after thirty-five years of Imamate.

قال الإمام علي بن الحسين عليهما السّلام :

«اتَّقُوا الْكَذِبَ الصَّغِيرَ مِنْهُ وَالْكَبِيرَ فِي كُلّ جِدّ وَ هَزْلٍ، فَإِنَّ الرَّجُلَ إذَا كَذِبَ فِي
الصَّغِيرِ اجْتَرَأَ عَلَى الْكَبِيرِ.

«لا يَخَافُ عَبْدٌ إلاَّ ذَنْبَهُ، وَلاَ يَرجُو إلاَّ رَبَّهُ، وَلاَ يَسْتَحِي الْجَاهِلُ إذَا سُئِلَ عَمَّا
لا يَعْلَمُ أنْ يَتَعَلَّمَ، وَالصَّبْرِ مِنَ الإِيمَانِ بِمَنْزِلَةِ الرَّأْسِ مِنَ الْجَسَدِ، وَلاَ إِيمَانَ لِمَنْ لاَ صَبْرَ لَهُ.

al-Imam `Ali ibn al-Husayn, peace be on him, said:

* Refrain from lying in all things, big or small, in
seriousness or in jest. For when one starts lying in petty
matters, soon he will have the audacity to lie in important

matters (also).

    * A man need not fear Allah except on account of his own sins, and should place his hopes only with his Lord. When about something one does not know, one should not be ashamed of having to learn about it. And patience is to faith what the head is to the body; one who does not have patience also lacks faith.

THE SEVENTH INFALLIBLE

THE FIFTH IMAM

THE BURIAL PLACE OF IMAM MUHAMMAD AL-BAQIR (A.S.)
JANNAT AL-BAQI', MEDINA.

MUHAMMAD IBN ALI AL-BAQIR
(Peace be on him)

Name: **Muhammad**
Title: al-Baqir.
Agnomen: Abu Ja'far.
Father's name: Ali Zaynu 'l-`Abidin.
Mother's name: Fatimah bint al-Hasan, known as Umm
  `Abdillah.
Birth: In Medina, on Tuesday, 1st *Rajab* 57 AH.
Death: Died at the age of 57, in Medina on Monday, 7th
  Dhi 'l-hijjah 114 AH; poisoned by Hisham ibn `Abdi
  'l-Malik; buried in Jannatu 'l-Baqi', in Medina.

THE HOLY Imam Muhammad al-Baqir is the Fifth Apostolic Imam. His epithet was Abu Ja'far and he was popularly titled "al-Baqir". His mother was the daughter of
Imam Hasan. Thus, he was the only Imam who was connected with Hadrat Fatimatu 'z-Zahra', both from his
paternal and maternal sides.

Imam Muhammad al-Baqir was brought up in the holy
lap of his grandfather Imam Husayn, for three years. For
thirty-four years he was under the gracious patronage of
his father, `Ali Zaynu 'l-`Abidin.

117

The Holy Imam was present in Karbala' at the time
of the gruesome tragedy of the wholesale massacre of
his grandfather Imam Husayn and his companions. He
also suffered with his father and the ladies of the House
of the Prophet (Ahlu 'l-bayt) the heartless captivity and
imprisonment at the hands of the devilish forces at the
command of Yazid ibn Mu'dwiyah. After the tragedy of
Karbala', the Imam passed his time peacefully in Medina
praying to Allah and guiding the people to the right path.

The downfall of the Umayyads had begun since
Yazid, the son of Mu'awiyah, had slaughtered Imam
Husayn. Yazid himself had completely realized the evil
consequences of his deeds even during the short period
of his rule. His son Mu'awiyah, the second, refused to
accept the caliphate saying

I cannot favour such a throne which has been erected
on the basis of oppression and tyranny.

Ibn Hajar al-Haytami, a famous scholar belonging to
the Sunnite School says: "Imam Muhammad   al-Baqir
has disclosed the secrets of knowledge and wisdom and
unfolded the principles of spiritual and religious guidance.
Nobody can deny his exalted character, his God-given
knowledge, his divinely-gifted wisdom and his obligation
and gratitude towards spreading of knowledge. He was
a sacred and highly talented spiritual leader and for this
reason he was popularly titled `al-Baqir' which means
`the exponder of knowledge'. Kind of heart, spotless
in character, sacred by soul and noble by nature, the
Imam devoted all his time in submission to Allah (and
in advocating the teachings of the Holy Prophet and
his descendants). It is beyond the power of a man to
count the deep impression of knowledge and guidance
left by the Imam on the hearts of the faithful. His sayings
in devotion and abstinence, in knowledge and wisdom,

and in religious exercise and submission to Allah are so great in number that the volume of this book is quite insufficient to cover them all." (*as-Sawa'iqu 'l-muhriqah*, p. 120)

The Holy Imam managed to collect the teachings and reforms of the Holy Prophet and his *Ahlu 'l-bayt* in the form of books. His pupils compiled books on different branches of science and arts under his instructions and guidance.

In the excellence of his personal purity and godly traits, the Holy Imam Muhammad al-Baqir was a model of the Holy Prophet and his great grandfather, `Ali ibn Abi Talib. His admonitions created a spiritual sensation among the Muslims in general. He was not only hospitable even to his worst enemies but also used to continually exhort them to the right path. He urged people to earn their livelihood by their own hard work.

The Holy Imam gave much importance to convening *majalis* (meetings) in commemoration of the martyrdom of Imam Husayn. Kumayt ibn Zayd al-Asadi, one of the most famous and highly talented poets of that time, used to recite the elegy of Imam Husayn in those *majalis*. Such type of *majalis* were also greatly encouraged by Imam Ja'far as-Sadiq and Imam `Ali ar-Rida, the Sixth and the Eighth Imams.

Imam Muhammad al-Baqir continued his preaching peacefully till 114 AH. On the 7th *Dhi 'l-hijjah* when he was fifty-seven years old, Hisham ibn `Abdi 'l-Malik ibn Marwan, the then ruler, got him martyred through poison. The funeral prayers for this Holy Imam were conducted by his son Imam Ja'far as-Sadiq, the Six Imam, and his body was laid to rest in Jannatu 'l-Baqi' in Medina.

al-`Allamah at-Tabataba'i writes:

Imam Muhammad ibn Ali al-Baqir (the word `baqir' meaning he who cuts and dissects, a title given to him by the Prophet) was the son of the Fourth Imam and was born in 57/675. He was present at the event of Karbala' when he was four years old. After his father, through Divine Command and the decree of those who went before him, he became Imam. In the year 114/732 he died, according to some Shiite traditions, he was poisoned by Ibrahim ibn al-Walid ibn `Abdillah, the nephew of Hisham, the Umayyad caliph.

During the Imamate of the Fifth Imam, as a result of the injustice of the Umayyads, revolts and wars broke out in some corner of the Islamic world every day. More over, there were disputes within the Umayyad family it-self which kept the caliphate busy and to a certain extent left the members of the Household of the Prophet alone. From the other side, the tragedy of Karbala' and the oppression suffered by the Household of the Prophet, of which the Fourth Imam was the most noteworthy embodiment, had attracted many Muslims to the Imam. These factors combined to make it possible for people and especially the Shiites to go in great numbers to Medina and to come into the presence of the Fifth Imam. Possibilities for disseminating the truth about Islam and the sciences of the Household of the Prophet, which had never existed for the Imams before him, were presented by the Fifth Imam. The proof of this fact is the innumerable traditions recounted from the Fifth Imam and the large number of illustrious men of science and Shi`ite scholars who were trained by him in different Islamic sciences. These names are listed in books of biographies of famous men in Islam. (Shi`ite Islam)

*   *   *   *   *

قال الإمام الباقر عليه السَّلام :

«الكَمَالُ ، كُلُّ الكَمَالِ التَّفقُهُ في الدِّينِ ، وَالصَّبْرُ عَلى ٱلنَّائِبَةِ ، وَتقدِيرُالْمَعِيشَةِ .

«عَالِمٌ يُنتَفَعُ بِعِلْمِهِ أَفضَلُ مِنْ سَبْعِينَ أَلْفِ عَابِدٍ .

«مَا عَرَفَ اللهَ مَنْ عَصَاهُ .

al-Imam al-Baqir, peace be on him, said:

* The height of perfection is excellence in the understanding of the religion, endurance in hardships and
administration of the affairs of life according to one's
means, in the right measure.

* The scholar (*'alim*) who derives benefit from his
knowledge is better than seventy thousand devotees
(*'abid*).

* One who disobeys Allah has no knowledge of Him.

THE EIGHTH INFALLIBLE

THE SIXTH IMAM

THE BURIAL PLACE OF IMAM JA'FAR AS-SADIQ (A.S.)
AT AL-BAQI', MEDINA.

JA'FAR IBN MUHAMMAD AS-SADIQ
(Peace be on him)

Name: **Ja'far**
Title: as-Sadiq.
Agnomen: Abu Abdillah.
Father's name: Muhammad al-Baqir.
Mother's name: Umm Farwah.
Birth: In Medina, on Monday, 17th *Rabi`u 'l-awwal* 83
   A.H.
Death: Died at the age of 65, in Medina on Monday, 25th
   Shawwal 148 AH; poisoned by al-Mansur ad-Dawa-
   niqi, the `Abbasid caliph.

THE HOLY Imam Ja'far as-Sadiq was the sixth in the
succession of the twelve Apostolic Imams. His epithet
was Abu `Abdillah and his famous titles were as-Sadiq,
al-Fadil and at-Tahir. He was the son of Imam Muhammad
al-Baqir, the Fifth Imam, and his mother was the daughter
of al-Qasim ibn Muhammad ibn Abi Bakr.

   Imam Ja'far as-Sadiq was brought up by his grandfather, Imam Zaynu '1- Abidin in Medina for twelve years
and then remained under the sacred patronage of his
father Imam Muhammad   al-Baqir for a period of nine-
teen years.

Imamate:

After the death of his holy father in 114 AH, he succeeded him as the Sixth Imam, and thus the sacred trust of Islamic mission and spiritual guidance was relayed down to his custody right from the Holy Prophet through the succession of the preceding Imams.

Political Condition:

The period of his Imamate coincided with the most revolutionary and eventful era of Islamic history which saw the downfall of the Umayyad Empire and the rise of the Abbasid caliphate. The internal wars and political upheavals were bringing about speedy reshufflements in government. Thus, the Holy Imam witnessed the reigns of various kings starting from `Abdu 'l-Malik down to the Umayyad ruler Marwan al-Himar. He further survived till the time of Abu 'l- Abbas as-Saffah and al-Mansur among the `Abbasids. It was due to the political strife between two groups viz., the Umayyads and `Abbasids for power that Imam was left alone undisturbed to carry out his devotional duties and peacefully carry on his mission to propagate Islam and spreading the teachings of the Holy Prophet.

In the last days of the Umayyad rule, their Empire was tottering and was on the verge of collapse, and a most chaotic and demoralized state of affairs prevailed throughout the Islamic State. The `Abbasids exploited such an opportunity and availing themselves of this political instability, assumed the title of "Avengers of Banu Hashim". They pretended to have stood for the cause of taking revenge on the Umayyads for shedding the innocent blood of the Holy Imam Husayn.

The common people who were groaning under the yoke of the Umayyads were fed up with their atrocities and were secretly yearning for the progeny of the Holy Prophet to take power. They realized that if the leadership went to the *Ahlu 'l-bayt,* who were its legitimate heir, the prestige of Islam would be enhanced and the Prophet's mission would be genuinely propagated. However, a group of the Abbdsids secretly dedicated their lives to a campaign for seizing power from the hands of the Umayyads on the pretext that they were seizing it only to surrender it to the Banu Hashim. Actually, they were plotting for their own ends. The common people were thus deceived into supporting them and when these 'Abbasids did succeed in snatching the power from the Umayyads, they turned against the *Ahlu 'l-bayt.*

Religious Condition:

The downfall of the Umayyads and the rise of the 'Abbasids constituted the two principal plots in the drama of Islamic history. This was a most chaotic and revolution ary period when the religious morals of Islam had gone down and the teachings of the Holy Prophet were being neglected, and a state of anarchy was rampant. It was amidst such deadly gloom that the virtuous personage of Imam Ja'far as-Sadiq stood like a beacon of light shedding its lustre to illuminate the ocean of sinful darkness around. The world got inclined towards his virtuous and admirable personality. Abu Salamah al-Khallal also offered him the throne of the caliphate. But the Imam keeping up the characteristic tradition of his ancestors flatly declined to accept it, and preferred to content himself with his devotional pursuits and service to Islam. On account of his many debates with the priests of rival orders like Atheists, Christians, Jews, etc.

Teachings:

The versatile genius of Imam Ja'far as-Sadiq in all branches of knowledge was acclaimed throughout the Islamic world, which attracted students from far-off places towards him till the strength of his disciples had reached four thousand. The scholars and experts in Divine Law have quoted many *ahadith* (traditions) from Imam Ja'far as-Sadiq. His disciples compiled hundred of books on various branches of science and arts. Other than *fiqh* (Islamic jurisprudence), *hadith* (tradition), *tafsir* (exegesis of the Holy Qur'an), etc., the Holy Imam also imparted mathematics and chemistry to some of his disciples. Jabir ibn Hayyan at-Tusi, a famous scholar of matehmatics, was one of the Imam's disciples who benefited from the Imam's knowledge and guidance and was able to write four hundred books on different subjects.

It is an undeniable historical truth that all the great scholars of Islam were indebted for their learning to the very presence of the *Ahlu 'l-bayt* who were the fountain of knowledge and learning for all.

al- Allamah ash-Shibli writes in his book *Siratu 'n-Nu`man:* "Abu Hanifah remained for a considerable period in the attendance of Imam Ja'far as-Sadiq, acquiring from him a great deal of precious research on *fiqh* and *hadith.* Both the sects - Shi'ah and Sunni - believe that the source of Abu Hanifah's knowledge was mostly derived from his association with Imam Ja'far as-Sadiq."

The Imam devoted his whole life to the cause of religious preaching and propagation of the teachings of the Holy Prophet and never strove for power. Because of his great knowledge and fine teaching, the people gathered around him, giving devotion and respect that was his due. This excited the envy of the Abbasid ruler al-Mansur ad-Dawaniqi, who fearing the popularity of the Imam, decided to do away with him.

al-`Allamah at-Tabataba'i writes:

Imam Ja'far ibn Muhammad, the son of the Fifth Imam, was born in 83/702. He died in 148/765 according to Shiite tradition, poisoned and martyred through the intrigue of the Abbasid caliph al-Mansur. After the death of his father he became Imam by Divine Command and decree of those who came before him.

During the Imamate of the Sixth Imam greater possibilities and a more favourable climate existed for him to propagate religious teachings. This came about as a result of revolts in Islamic lands, especially the uprising of the Muswaddah to overthrow the Umayyad caliphate, and the bloody wars which finally led to the fall and extinction of the Umayyads. The greater opportunities for Shiite teachings were also a result of the favourable ground the Fifth Imam had prepared during the twenty years of his Imamate through the propagation of the true teachings of Islam and the sciences of the Household of the Prophet.

The Imam took advantage of the occasion to propagate the religious sciences until the very end of his Imamate, which was contemporary with the end of the Umayyad and beginning of the Abbasid caliphates. He instructed many scholars in different fields of the intellectual and transmitted sciences, such as Zurarah ibn A'yan, Muhammad ibn Muslim, Muminu 't-Taq, Hisham ibn al-Hakam, Aban ibn Taghlib, Hisham ibn Salim, Hurayz, Hisham al-Kalbi an-Nassabah and Jabir ibn Hayyan (the alchemist). Even some important Sunni scholars such as Sufyan ath-Thawri, Abu Hanifah, the founder of the Hanafi school of law, al-Qadi as-Sukuni, al-Qadi Abu '1-Bakhtari, and others, had the honour of being his students. It is said that his classes and sessions of instructions produced four thousand scholars of *hadith* and other sciences. The number of traditions preserved from the Fifth and Sixth Imams is more than all the *hadith* that have been recorded from the Prophet and the other ten Imams combined.

But toward the end of his life the Imam was subjected to severe restrictions placed upon him by the `Abbasid caliph al-Mansur, who ordered such torture and merciless killing of many of the descendants of the Prophet who were Shi`ite that his actions even surpassed the cruelty and heedlessness of the Umayyads. At his order they were arrested in groups, some thrown into deep and dark prisons and tortured until they died, while others were beheaded or buried alive or placed at the base of or between walls of buildings, and walls were constructed over them.

Hisham, the Umayyad caliph, had ordered the Sixth Imam to be arrested and brought to Damascus. Later, the Imam was arrested by as-Saffah, the Abbasid caliph, and brought to Iraq. Finally, al-Mansur had him arrested again and brought to Samarrah where he had the Imam kept under supervision, was in every way harsh and discourteous to him, and several times thought of killing him. Eventually the Imam was allowed to return to Medina where he spent the rest of his life in hiding, until he was poisoned and martyred through the intrigue of al-Mansur.

Upon hearing the news of the Imam's martyrdom, al-Mansur wrote to the governor of Medina instructing him to go to the house of the Imam on the pretext of expressing his condolences to the family, to ask for the Imam's will and testament and read it. Whoever was chosen by the Imam as his inheritor and successor should be beheaded on the spot. Of course, the aim of al-Mansur was to put an end to the whole question of the Imamate and to Shl'ite aspirations. When the governor of Medina, following orders, read the last will and testament, he saw

that the Imam had chosen four people rather than one
to administer his last will and testament: the caliph himself, the governor of Medina, `Abdullah Aftah, the Imam's
older son, and Musa, his younger son. In this way the plot
of al-Mansur failed. (*Shi`ite Islam*)

Death:

On 25th *Shawwal* 148 AH, the governor of Medina
by the order of al-Mansur, got the Imam martyred through
poison. The funeral prayer was conducted by his son Imam
Musa al-Kazim, the Seventh Imam, and his body was laid
to rest in the cemetery of Jannatu 'l-Baqi'.

قال الإمام الصّادق عليه السّلام :

«إنَّ خَيْرَالْعِبَادِ مَنْ تَجْتَمِعُ فِيهِ خَمْسُ خِصَالٍ : إذَا أَحْسَنَ اسْتَبْشَرَ، وَ إذَا أَسَاءَ
اسْتَغْفَرَ، وَ إذَا أُعْطِيَ (من الله شيئا) شَكَرَ، وَ إذَا أَبْلِيَ (من الله) صَبَرَ، وَ إذَا ظُلِمَ غَفَرَ.

«ثَلاثَةٌ لاَ يَزِيدُ اللهُ بِهَا الْمَرْءَ الْمُسْلِمَ إلاَّ عِزًّا : الصَّفْحُ عَمَّنْ ظَلَمَهُ، وَالإعطَاءُ لِمَنْ
حَرَمَهُ، وَالصِّلَةُ لِمَنْ قَطَعَهُ.

«ألْمُؤْمِنُ إذَا غَضِبَ لَمْ يُخْرِجْهُ غَضَبُهُ مِنْ حَقٍّ، وَ إذَا رَضِيَ لَمْ يُدْخِلْهُ رِضَاهُ فِي
بَاطِلٍ، وَ إذَا قَدِرَ لَمْ يَأْخُذْ أَكْثَرَ مِمَّا لَهُ.

al-Imam as-Sadiq, peace be on him, said:

   * One who has these five characteristics is the choicest
of men: one who feels joyous when he does something
good; one who repents when he does something bad; one
who is grateful when he receives something from Allah;
one who patiently endures Allah's trials; one who forgives
when he is done some injustice or wrong.

closer to Allah: forgiving one who has wronged him; being generous to one who had deprived him; being kind to a kinsman who has not observed his rights of kinship.

   * The true believer does not transgress the limits of fairness in a fit of anger; he does not do anything unjustifiable for the sake of favour to some; neither does he take   more than his due share, though he may have the power.

THE NINTH INFALLIBLE

THE SEVENTH IMAM

THE HOLY SHRINE OF IMAM MUSA AL-KAZIM (A.S.)
AT AL-KAZIMIYYAH, BAGHDAD.

MUSA IBN JA'FAR AL-KAZIM
(Peace be on him)

Name: **Musa**
Title: al-Kazim.
Agnomen: Abu Ibrahim.
Father's name: Ja'far as-Sadiq.
Mother's name: Hamidah al-Barbariyyah.
Birth: In Abwa' (between Mecca and Medina) on Sunday,
 7th *Safar* 128 AH.
Death: Died at the age of 55, in Baghdad, on 25th *Rajab*
 183 AH; poisoned by Harun ar-Rashid; buried in al-
 Kazimiyyah, Baghdad.

THE HOLY Imam Musa al-Kazim is the Seventh Apostolic Imam. His epithet was Abu 'l-Hasan and his famous
title was al-Kazim. His matchless devotion and worship
of God has also earned him the title of " al-'abdu 's-Salih"
(virtuous slave of God). Generosity was synonymous
with his name and no beggar ever returned from his door
empty handed. Even after his death, he continued to be
obliging and was generous to his devotees who came to
his holy tomb with prayers and behests which were invari-
ably granted by God. Thus, one of his additional titles is
also "Babu 'l-Hawaij" (the door to fulfilling needs).

Parents:

The Holy Imam Musa al-Kazim was the son of Imam Ja'far as-Sadicl, the Sixth Imam. The name of his mother was Hamidah, the daughter of a noble man hailing from the States of Barbary.

Childhood:

Imam Musa al-Kazim passed twenty years of his sacred life under the gracious patronage of his holy father. His inherent genius and gifted virtues combined with the enlightened guidance and education from the Holy Imam Ja'far as-Sadiq, showed in the manifestation of his future personality. He was fully versed with the Divine Knowledge even in his childhood.

al-`Allamah al-Majlisi relates that once Abu Hanifah happened to call upon the holy abode of Imam Ja'far as-Sadiq to ask him about some religious matters (masa 'il). The Imam was asleep and so he kept waiting outside till the Imam's awakening. Meanwhile, Imam Musa al-Kazim, who was then five years old, came out of his house. Abu Hanifah, after offering him his best compliments, enquired:

"O the son of the Holy Prophet! what is your opinion about the deeds of a man? Does he do them by himself or does God make him do them?"

"O Abu Hanifah", the five years old Imam replied at once, in the typical tone of his ancestors, "the doings of a man are confined to three possibilities. First, that God alone does them while the man is quite helpless. Second, that both God and the man do equally share the commitment. Third, that man does them alone. Now, if the first assumption is true, it obviously proves the un-justness of God who punishes His creatures for sins which they have not committed. And if the second condition be acceptable, even then God becomes unjust if He punishes the man for the crimes in which He is equally a partner. But the undesirability of both these conditions is evident in the case of God. Thus, we are naturally left with the third alternative to the problem that men are absolutely responsible for their own doings."

Imamate:

The Holy Imam Ja'far as-Sadiq breathed his last on 25th Shawwdl 148 AH, and with effect from the same date Imam Musa al-Kazim succeeded the holy office of Imamate as the Seventh Imam. The period of his Imamate continued for thirty-five years. In the first decade of his Imamate, Imam Musa al-Kazim could afford a peaceful execution of the responsibilities of his sacred office and carried on the propagation of the teachings of the Holy Prophet. But soon after, he fell a victim to the ruling kings and a greater part of his life passed in prison.

Political Condition:

Imam Musa al-Kazim lived under the most crucial times in the regimes of the despotic `Abbasid kings who were marked for their tyrannical and cruel administration. He witnessed the reigns of al-Mansur ad-Dawaniqi, al-Mahdi and Harun ar-Rashid. al-Mansur and Harun ar-Rashid were the despotic kings who put a multitude of innocent descendants of the Holy Prophet to the sword. Thousands of these martyrs were buried alive inside walls or put into horrible dark prisons during their lifetime. These depraved caliphs knew no pity or justice and they killed and tortured for the pleasure they derived from human sufferings.

The Holy Imam was saved from the tyranny of al-Mansur because the king, being occupied with his project of constructing the new city of Baghdad, could not get time to turn towards victimizing the Imam. By 157 AH the city of Baghdad was built. This was soon followed by the death of its founder a year later. After al-Mansur, his son al-Mahdi ascended the throne. For a few years he remained indifferent towards the Imam. When in 164 AH he came to Medina and heard about the great reputation of the Imam, he could not resist his jealousy and the spark of his ancestral malice against the Ahlu 'l-bayt was rekindled. He somehow managed to take the Imam along with him to Baghdad and got him imprisoned there. But after a year he realized his mistake and released the Imam from jail. al-Mahdi was succeeded by al-Hadi who lived only for a year. Now, in 170 AH, the most cruel and tyrannical king Harun ar-Rashid appeared at the head of the `Abbasid Empire. It was during his reign that the Holy Imam passed the greater part of his life in a miserable prison till he was poisoned.

Moral and Ethical Excellence:

As regards his morality and ethical excellence, Ibn Hajar al-Haytami remarks: "The patience and forbearance of Imam Musa al-Kazim was such that he was given the title of `al-Kazim' (one who swallows down his anger). He was the embodiment of virtue and generosity. He devoted his nights to the prayers of God and his days to fasting. He always forgave those who did wrong to him."

His kind and generous attitude towards the people was such that he used to patronize and help the poor and destitutes of Medina and provide for them cash, food, clothes and other necessitities of sustenance secretly. It continued to be a riddle for the receivers of gifts throughout the Imam's lifetime as to who their benefactor was, but the secret was not revealed until after his death.

Literary Attainments:

Time and circumstances did not permit the Holy Imam Musa al-Kazim to establish institutions to impart religious knowledge to his followers as his father, Imam Ja'far as-Sadiq and his grandfather, Imam Muhammad al-Baqir had done. He was never allowed to address a congregation. He carried on his mission of preaching and guiding people quietly.

Death:

In 179 AH, Harun ar-Rashid visited Medina. The fire of malice and jealousy against the *Ahlu 'l-bayt* was kindled in his heart when he saw the great influence and popularity which the Holy Imam enjoyed amongst the people there. He got the Imam arrested while he was busy in prayer at the tomb of the Holy Prophet and kept him in prison in Baghdad for a period of about four years. On the 25th *Rajab* 183 AH, he got the Imam martyred by poison. Even his corpse was not spared humiliation and was taken out of the prison and left on the Bridge of Baghdad. His devotees, however, managed to lay the holy body of the Imam to rest in al-Kazimiyyah (Iraq).

قال الامام الكاظمُ عليه السَّلام

• عَوْنُكَ للضَّعِيفِ مِنْ أفضَل الصَّدَقَةِ

• ألزَمُ العِلم لَكَ مَادَلَّكَ عَلَى صَلاح قَلْبِكَ وَأظهَرَ لَكَ فَسَادَهُ.

• لاَ تَشْغَلَنَّ بِعلم مَا لاَ يَضُرُّكَ جَهْلُهُ، وَلاَ تَغْفُلَنَّ عَنْ عِلم مَا يَزيدُ في جَهْلِكَ تَرْكُهُ.

al-Imam al-Kazim, peace be on him, said:

* No charity is superior to giving a helping hand to the weak.

* Never bother to learn something not knowing which does not do you any harm, and never neglect to learn something whose negligence will increase your ignorance.

THE TENTH INFALLIBLE

THE EIGHTH IMAM

THE HOLY SHRINE OF IMAM `ALI AR-RIDA (A.S.)
AT MASHHAD (IRAN).

`ALI IBN MUSA AR-RIDA
(Peace be on him)

Name: `Ali.

Title: ar-Rida.

Agnomen: Abu 'l-Hasan.

Father's name: Musa al-Kazim.

Mother's name: Ummu 'l-Banin Najmah.

Birth: In Medina, on Thursday, 11th *Dhu 'l-qi'dah* 148 A H.

Death: Died at the age of 55, in Mashhad (Khurasan), on Tuesday, 17th *Safar* 203 AH; poisoned by al-Ma'mun, the Abbasid caliph; buried in Mashhad, Iran.

IMAM ALI ar-Rida was brought up under the holy guidance of his father for thirty-five years. His own insight and brilliance in religious matters combined with the excellent training and education given by his father made him unique in his spiritual leadership. Imam ar-Rida was a living example of the piety of the great Prophet and the chivalry and generosity of Imam `Ali ibn Abi Talib.

Succession:

Imam Musa al-Kazim was well aware of the aggressive designs of the government in power against the Imamate and therefore, during his lifetime he declared Imam ar-Rida as his successor in the presence of hundred and seventy-one prominent religious divines and called upon his sons and his family to submit to him and refer to him in all matters after him. He also left behind a written document declaring the succession of Imam ar-Rida duly signed and endorsed by not less than sixteen prominent persons. All these necessary steps were taken by the great Imam to avoid any confusion that may have arisen after his death.

Imamate:

Imam Musa al-Kazim was poisoned while he was still in prison and expired on 25th *Rajab 183* AH, and on the same day Imam ar-Rida was declared as the Eighth Imam of the Muslim world. Imam ar-Rida had the great task before him of coming out with the correct interpretation of the Holy Qur'an; specially under the most unfavourable circumstances prevailing under the government of Harun ar-Rashid. Many belonging to the faith were imprisoned and those who were free and could not be jailed faced untold atrocities and sufferings. Imam ar-Rida, of course, stamped his impression upon his age by carrying on the mission of the Great Prophet in a peaceful manner even during the most chaotic periods, and it was mostly due to his efforts that the teachings of the Holy Prophet and his descendants became widespread.

Imam ar-Rida had inherited great qualities of head and heart from his ancestors. He was a versatile person and had full command over many languages. Ibnu 'l-Athir al-Jazari penned very rightly that Imam ar-Rida was undoubtedly the greatest sage, saint and scholar of the second century (AH).

Once, on his way to Khurasan, when he (the Imam) was brought by force by the guards of al-Ma'mun from Medina, he arrived on horseback at Naysabur. Myriads of people gathered round him and all roads were over-crowded as they had come to meet and see their great Imam. Abu Dhar'ah ar-Razi and Muhammad ibn Aslam at-Tusi, the two great scholars of the day, stepped out of the crowd and begged the Imam to halt there for a moment so that the faithful may be able to hear his voice. They also requested the Imam to address the gathering. The Imam granted the request and in his brief address told the mammoth gathering the real interpretation of *la ilaha illa Allah.* Quoting Allah, he continued to say that the *kalimah* is the fortress of Allah and whoever entered the fortress saved himself from His wrath.

He paused for a moment and continued that there were also a few conditions to entitle the entrance to the fortress and the greatest of all conditions was sincere and complete submission to the Imam of the day; and very boldly and frankly explained to the people that any disloyalty to the Prophet and his descendants would withdraw the right of the entrance to the fortress. The only way to earn Almighty Allah's pleasure was to obey the Prophet and his progeny and that was the only path to salvation and immortality.

The above-mentioned incident speaks clearly of the great popularity of Imam ar-Rida, and the love, loyalty and respect the Muslims gave their beloved Imam. al-Ma'mun, the king, was conscious of the fact that he would not survive for long if he also did not express his loyalty to the great leader and his intelligence department had made it clear to him that the Iranian people were truly and sincerely loyal to the Imam and he could only win them over if he also pretended to give respect and sympathetic consideration to Imam `Ali ar-Rida. al-Ma'mun was a very shrewd person. He made a plan to invite Imam ar-Rida and to offer him the heirship to the throne. The Imam was summoned by a royal decree and was compelled, under the circumstances, to leave Medina - where he was living a quiet life - and present himself at the royal court of al-Ma'mun.

On his arrival, al-Ma'mun showed him hospitality and great respect, then he said to him: "I want to get rid of myself of the caliphate and vest the office in you." But ar-Rida refused his offer. Then al-Ma'mun r0peated his offer in a letter saying: "If you refuse what I have offered you, then you must accept being the heir after me." But again ar-Rida refused his offer vigorously. al-Ma'mun summoned him. He was alone with al-Fadl ibn Sahl, the man with two offices (i.e., military and civil). There was no one else in their gathering. al-Ma'mun said to ar-Rida, "I thought it appropriate to invest authority over the Muslims in you and to relieve myself of the responsibility by giving it to you." When again ar-Rida refused to accept his offer, al-Ma'mun spoke to him as if threatening him for his refusal. In his speech he said, " 'Umar ibn al-Khattab made a committee of consultation (shirá) (to appoint a successor). Among them was your forefather, the Commander of the faithful, `Ali ibn Abi Talib. (`Umar) stipulated that any of them who opposed the decision should be executed. So there is no escape for you from accepting what I want from you. I will ignore your rejection of it."

In reply, ar-Rida said: "I will agree to what you want of me as far as succession is concerned on condition that I do not command, nor order, nor give legal decisions, nor judge, nor appoint, nor dismiss, nor change anything from how it is at present." al-Ma'mun accepted all of that.

On the day when al-Ma'mun ordered to make the pledge of allegiance to ar-Rida, one of the close associates of ar-Rida, who was present, narrates, "On that day I was in front of him. He looked at me while I was feeling happy about what had happened. He signalled me to come closer. I went closer to him and he said so that no one else could hear, `Do not occupy your heart with this matter and do not be happy about it. It is something which will not be achieved.' "

Quoting al-`Allamah ash- Shibli from his book *al-Ma'mun*, we get a very clear picture of how al-Ma'mun decided to offer his leadership to Imam ar-Rida.

"Imam ar-Rida was the Eighth Imam and al-Ma'mfrn could not help holding him in great esteem because of the Imam's piety, wisdom, knowledge, modesty, decorum and personality. Therefore, he decided to nominate him as the rightful heir to the throne. Earlier in 200 AH he had summoned the Abbasids. Thirty-three thousand `Abbasids responded to the invitation and were entertained as royal guests. During their stay at the capital he very closely observed and noted their capabilities and eventually arrived at the conclusion that not one of them deserved to succeed him. He therefore spoke to them all in an assembly in 201 AH telling them in categorical terms that none of the `Abbasids deserved to succeed him. He demanded allegiance to Imam ar-Rida from the people in this very meeting and declared that royal robes would be green in future, the colour which had the unique distinction of being that of the Imam's dress. A Royal decree was published saying that Imam ar-Rida will succeed al-Ma'mun.

Even after the declaration of succession when there was every opportunity for the Imam to live a splendid worldly royal life, he did not pay any heed to material comforts and devoted himself completely to imparting the true Islamic conception of the Prophet's teachings and the Holy Qur'an. He spent most of his time praying to God and serving the people.

Taking full advantage of the concessions given to him by virtue of his elevated position in the royal court, he organized the majdlis (meetings) commemorating the martyrdom of the martyrs of Karbala'. These majdlis were first held during the days of Imam Muhammad al-Baqir and Imam Ja'far as-Sadiq, but Imam ar-Rida gave the majdlis a new impetus by encouraging those poets who wrote effective poems depicting the moral aspects of the tragedy and the suffering of Imam Husayn and his companions.

al-Ma'mun had been very scared of the growing popularity of the Imam and he had appointed him as his heir to the throne only for the fulfilment of his own most ambitious and sinister designs and getting the Imam's endorsement to his tricky plans. But the Imam naturally refused to give his endorsement to any such plans which were against the teaching of Islam. al-Ma'mun therefore became very disappointed with him and decided once and for all to check his growing popularity and ensuring his own survival by acting according to the old traditions of killing the Imam. Wanting to do it in a more subtle manner, he invited the Imam to dinner, and fed him poisoned grapes. The Imam died on 17th Safar 203 AH, he was buried in Tus (Mashhad) and his Grand Shrine speaks well for the great personality the Imam possessed. Myriads of Muslims visit his Shrine every year to pay their homage to this Imam.

قال الإمام الرِّضا عليه السَّلام :

«سَبْعَةُ أَشْيَاءَ بِغَيْرِ سَبْعَةِ أَشْيَاءَ مِنَ الاسْتِهْزَاءِ : مَنِ أسْتَغْفَرَ بِلِسَانِهِ وَ لَمْ يَنْدَمْ بِقَلْبِهِ
فَقَدِ أسْتَهْزَأَ بِنَفْسِهِ ، وَ مَنْ سَأَلَ اللهَ التَّوْفِيقَ وَ لَمْ يَجْتَهِدْ فَقَدِ أسْتَهْزَأَ بِنَفْسِهِ ، وَ مَنْ أسْتَحْزَمَ
(اِدَّعى الحَزْمِ ، أي العقل والبصيرة) وَ لَمْ يَحْذَرْ فَقَدِ أسْتَهْزَأَ بِنَفْسِهِ ، وَ مَنْ سَأَلَ اللهَ الْجَنَّةَ
وَ لَمْ يَصْبِرْ عَلَى الشَّدَائِدِ فَقَدِ أسْتَهْزَأَ بِنَفْسِهِ ، وَ مَنْ تَعَوَّذَ بِاللهِ مِنَ النَّارِ وَلَمْ يَتْرُكِ الشَّهَوَاتِ
فَقَدِ أسْتَهْزَأَ بِنَفْسِهِ ، وَ مَنْ ذَكَرَاللهَ وَ لَمْ يَسْتَبِقْ إلى لِقَائِهِ فَقَدِ أسْتَهْزَأَ بِنَفْسِهِ .

al-Imam ar-Rida, peace be on him, said:

* Doing seven things without doing the seven other things is self-mockery: asking for forgiveness from Allah verbally without repenting with the heart; asking for Allah's help without undertaking any effort; making a firm resolution to do something without taking due precautions; asking Allah for Paradise without enduring the related hardships; beseeching deliverance from the Hell-fire without refraining from lusts; remembering Allah without anticipating to encounter Him.

THE ELEVENTH INFALLIBLE

THE NINTH IMAM

THE HOLY SHRINE OF IMAM MUHAMMAD AL-JAWAD (A.S.)
AT AL-KAZIMIYYAH, BAGHDAD.

MUHAMMAD IBN ALI AL-JAWAD (AT-TAQI)
(Peace be on him)

Name: **Muhammad**
Title: al-Jawad or at-Taqi.
Agnomen: Abu Ja'far.
Father's name: `Ali ar-Rida.
Mother's name: Sabikah (or Khayzuran).
Birth: In Medina, on Friday, 10th *Rajab* 195 AH.
Death: Died at the age of 25, in al-Kazimiyyah on Wednes-
day, 29th *Dhi 'l-qi'dah* 220 AH, poisoned by Mu'ta-
sim, the `Abbasid caliph; buried in al-Kazimiyyah,
Baghdad.

IMAM MUHAMMAD al-Jawad (or at-Taqi) is the Ninth
Apostolic Imam. His epithet was Abu Ja'far and his famous
titles were al-Jawad and at-Taqi. Since Imam Muhammad
al-Baqir, the Fith Imam was called Abu Ja'far, historians
have mentioned this Imam as Abu Ja'far the Second.

Childhood:
Imam Muhammad al-Jawad was brought up by his
Holy father Imam `Ali ar-Rida for four years. Under the
force of circumstances Imam `Ali ar-Rida had to migrate

from Medina to Khurasan (Iran), leaving his young son behind him. The Imam was fully aware of the treacherous character of the ruling king and was sure that he would return to Medina no more. So before his departure from Medina he declared his son Muhammad al-Jawad as his successor, and imparted to him . all his stores of Divine knowledge and spiritual genius.

Imamate:

Imam `Ali ar-Rida was poisoned on 17th *Safar* 203 AH and with effect from the same date Imam Muhammad al-Jawad was commissioned by Allah to hold the responsi bility of Imamate. At the tender age of eight there was no apparent chance or means of the young Imam reaching great heights of knowledge and practical achievements. But after a few days he is known not only to have debated with his contemporary scholars on subjects pertaining to *fiqh* (Islamic jurisprudence), *hadith* (tradition), *tafsir* (Qur'anic exegesis), etc. and outwitted them, but also to exhort their admiration and acknowledgment of his learning and superiority. Right from then the world realized that he possessed Divine knowledge and that the knowledge commanded by the Holy Imam was not acquired, but granted by Allah.

Literary Attainments and Excellence:

The span of the life of Imam Muhammad al-Jawad was shorter than that of his predecessors as well as his successors. He became Imam at the age of eight years and was poisoned at the age of twenty-five; yet his literary attainments were many and he commanded great respect and esteem.

The Holy Imam al-Jawad was the symbol of Prophet Muhammad's affability and Imam `Ali's attainments.

His hereditary qualities comprised of gallantry, boldness, charity, learning, forgiveness and tolerance. The brightest and most outstanding phases of his nature and character were to show hospitality and courtesy to all without discrimination, to help the needy; to observe equality under all circumstances, to live a simple life; to help the orphans, the poor and the homeless; to impart learning to those interested in the acquisition of knowledge and guide the people to the right path.

Migration to Iraq:

For the consolidation of his empire, it was realized by al-Ma'mun, the `Abbasid king, that it was necessary to win the sympathy and support of the Iranians who had always been friendly to the Ahlu 'l-bayt. Consequently, al-Ma'mun was forced, from a political point of view, to establish contacts with the tribe of Banu Fatimah at the expense of the ties with Banu Abbas and thereby win the favour of the Shi'ah. Accordingly, he declared Imam `Ali ar-Rida as his heir even against the Imam's will and got his sister Umm Habibah marrried to him. al-Ma'mun expected that Imam Ali ar-Rida would lend him his support in political affairs of the State. But when he discovered that the Imam was little interested in political matters and that the masses were more and more submitting themselves to him due to his spiritual greatness, he got him poisoned. Yet the exigency which directed him to nominate Imam `Ali ar-Rida as his heir and successor still continued. Hence he desired to marry his daughter  Ummu 'l-Fadl to Muhammad al-Jawad, the son of Imam `Ali ar-Rida and with this object in view, he summoned the Imam from Medina to Iraq.

The Banu `Abbas were extremely disconcerted when they came to know that al-Ma'mun was planning to marry his daughter to Imam Muhammad al-Jawad. A delegation of some leading persons waited on him in order to dissuade him from his intention. But al-Ma'mun continued to admire the learning and excellence of the Imam. He would say that though Imam Muhammad al-Jawad was still young, yet he was a true successor to his father in all his virtues and that the profoundest scholars of the Islamic world could not compete with him. When the Abbasids noticed that al-Ma'mun attributed the Imam's superiority to his learning they chose Yahya ibn Aktham, the greatest scholar and jurist of Baghdad, to contend with him.

al-Ma'mun issued a proclamation and organized a grand meeting for the contest which resulted in a huge gathering of people from all parts of the kingdom. Apart from noble and high officials, there were as many as nine hundred chairs reserved for scholars and learned men only. The world wondered how a young child could contest with the veteran judge in religious laws (*qadi 'l-qudat)* and the greatest scholar of Iraq.

Imam Muhammad al-Jawad was seated beside al-Ma'mun on his throne face to face with Yahya ibn Aktham, who addressed the Imam thus:

"Do you permit me to ask you a question? "

"Ask me whatever you wish," said the Imam in the typical tone of his ancestors.

Yahya then asked the Imam, "What is your verdict about a man who indulges in hunting while he is in the state of ihrdm." (In the code of religious law hunting is supposed to be forbidden for a pilgrim.)

The Imam at once replied, "Your question is vague and misleading. You should have definitely mentioned whether he hunted within the jurisdiction of the Ka'bah or outside; whether he was literate or illiterate; whether he was a slave or a free citizen; whether he was a minor or a major; whether it was for the first time or he had done it previously; also whether, that victim was a bird or some other creature; whether the prey was small or big; whether he hunted in the day or at night; whether the hunter repented for his action or persisted in it; whether he hunted secretly or openly; whether the *ihram* was for *umrah* or for *hajj*. Unless all these points are explained no specific answer can be given to this question."

al-Qadi Yahya was staggered in listening to these words of the Imam and the entire gathering was dumbfounded. There was no limit to al-Ma'mun's pleasure. He expressed his sentiments of joy and admiration thus, "Bravo! well done! O Abu Ja'far! (*Ahsanta, ahsanta ya Aba Ja'far*), your learning and attainments are beyond all praises."

As al-Ma'mun wanted that the Imam's opponent be fully exposed, he said to the Imam, "You may also put some question to Yahya ibn Aktham."

Then Yahya also reluctantly said to the Imam, "Yes, you may ask me some questions. If I know the answer, I will tell it; otherwise, I shall request you to give its answer."

Thereupon, the Imam asked a question to which Yahya could not reply. Eventually, the Imam answered his question.

Then al-Ma'mun addressed the audience thus: "Did I not say that the Imam comes of a family which has been chosen by Allah as the repository of knowledge and learning? Is there any one in the world who can match even the children of this family? "

All of them shouted, "Undoubtedly there is no one parallel to Muhammad ibn `Ali al-Jawad."

In the same assembly al-Ma'mun wedded his daughter Ummu 'l-Fadl to the Imam and liberally distributed

charity and gifts among his subjects as a mark of rejoicing.
One year after his marriage the Imam returned to Medina
from Baghdad with his wife and there he set about preaching the Commandments of Allah.

Death:

When after the death of al-Ma'mun, al-Mu'tasim ascended the throne, he got an opportunity to persecute
the Imam and to ventilate spite and malice against him.
He summoned the Imam to Baghdad. The Imam arrived
at Baghdad on 9th *Muharram* 220 AH and al-Mu'tasim
got him poisoned in the same year. He died on 29th *Dhi 'l-
qi'dah* 220 AH and was buried beside his grandfather,
Imam Musa al-Kazim the Seventh Imam, in al-Kazimiyyah, in the suburb of Baghdad (Iraq).

*　　*　　*

. قَالَ الاِمامُ الجَوادُ عليهِ السَّلام

ه أَلثِّقَةُ بِأللهِ ثَمَنٌ لِكُلِّ غَالٍ وَ سُلَّمٌ إِلَى كُلِّ عَالٍ .

ه مَنْ أَطَاعَ هَوَاهُ أَعْطَى عَدُوَّهُ مُنَاهُ .

ه لاَ تَكُنْ وَلِيّاً لِلّٰهِ فِي الْعَلاَنِيَةِ وَ عَدُوّاً لَهُ فِي ألسِّرِّ .

al-Imam al-Jawad, peace be on him, said:

* The trust in Allah is the price of everything that is
precious and the ladder to every goal which is high and
sublime.

* One who follows his desires, concedes to the wishes
of his enemy.

* Do not be an apparent friend of Allah in open and
a secret enemy of His in private.

THE TWELFTH INFALLIBLE

THE TENTH IMAM

THE HOLY SHRINE OF IMAM `ALI AL-HADI (A.S.)
AT SAMARRA' (IRAQ).

ALI IBN MUHAMMAD AL-HADI (AN-NAQI)
(Peace be on him)

Name: **Ali**.
Title: al-Hadi or an-Naqi.
Agnomen: Abu 'l-Hasan.
Father's name: Muhammad al-Jawad (at-Taqi).
Mother's name: Sumanah.
Birth: In Suryah (in the environs of Medina), on Friday,
2nd *Rajab,* 212 AH.
Death: Died at the age of 42, in Samarra, on Monday,
26th *Jumada 'th-thaniyah* 254 AH; poisoned by al-
Mu'tazz, the `Abbasid caliph; buried in Samarra';
North of Baghdad (Iraq).

THE TENTH Holy Imam, like his father, was also elevated
to the rank of Imam in his childhood. He was six years old
when his father Imam Muhammad al-Jawad died. After
the death of al-Ma'mun, al-Mu'tasim succeeded him, and
was later followed by the caliph al-Wathiq. In the first
five years of the reign of al-Wathiq, Imam `Ali al-Hadi
(an-Naqi) lived peacefully. After al-Wathiq, al-Mutawakkil came to power. Being too occupied in State affairs,
al-Mutawakkil did not get any time to harass the Imam

and his followers for four years. But as soon as he freed himself from State affairs, he started to molest the Imam. The Holy Imam devoted himself to the sacred mission of preaching in Medina and did thus earn the faith of the people as well as their allegiance and recognition of his great knowledge and attributes. This reputation of the Imam evoked the jealousy and malice of al-Mutawakkil against him.

The governor of Medina wrote to al-Mutawakkil that Imam Ali al-Hadi had been manoeuvring a coup against the government and a multitude of Shiites were pledged to his support. Although enraged by this news al-Mutawakkil still preferred the diplomacy of not arresting the Holy Imam. Under the garb of pretended respect and love towards the Imam, he planned to put him under life imprisonment after inviting him to his palace.

Prior to his imprisonment, in a series of correspondence with the Imam, he expressed the view that he was convinced of all the claims of the Imam and was ready to settle them amicably. He wrote to the Imam that having been acquainted with his great personality, his matchless knowledge and his peerless attributes, he was impatiently looking forward to the honour of seeing him, and he most cordially invited him to Samarra'. Although the Imam was well aware of al-Mutawakkil's treacherous intentions, he anticipating the fatal consequences of refusing the offer, reluctantly decided to leave Medina. But when the Imam arrived at Samarra' and al-Mutawakkil was informed about it, he took no notice of the Imam's arrival. When asked about where the Imam should stay, he ordered that the Imam should be put up in the inn meant for beggars, destitutes and homeless people.

al-Mutawakkil who was a deadly enemy of the Ahlu 'l-bayt, removed the Imam from this inn and entrusted him to the custody of a stone-hearted brute named Zurafah. But, by the grace of Allah, his enmity was, in a short time, transformed into love and devotion for the Imam. When al-Mutawakkil learnt about it, he shifted the Imam into the custody of another cruel man called Said. The Imam remained under his strict vigilance for a number of years, during which he was subjected to boundless tortures. But even in this miserable imprisonment, the Imam kept devoting himself at all times to the worship of Allah. The watchman of the prison used to comment that Imam Ali al-Hadi seemed to be an angel in human garb.

When Fat-h ibn Khaqan became the vizier of al-Mutawakkil, he being a Shi'ah could not stand the idea of the Imam's captivity. He endeavoured to have him released from imprisonment and arranged for his comfortable residence in a personally purchased house at Samarra'. Still al-Mutawakkil could hardly refrain from his antagonism to the Imam and he appointed spies to watch the Imam and his connections. But, through all these attempts, his hope of creating some fabrication to prove the Imam's activity against himself could not be realized.

In the time of al-Mutawakkil there was a woman named Zaynab who claimed to be a descendant of Imam Husayn. al-Mutawakkil sought the confirmation of Zaynab's claim from the Imam and said: "That as the beasts are prohibited to eat the flesh of the descendants of Imam Husayn he would throw Zaynab to the beasts and test her claim." On hearing this, Zaynab began to tremble and confessed that she was a fake. al-Mutawakkil then ordered the Imam to be thrown to the beasts to test the claim. To his great surprise, he witnessed the beasts prostrating their heads before the Imam.

Once al-Mutawakkil happened to suffer from a serious

malady which was eventually declared incurable by his physicians. When the Imam was approached for some remedy, he prescribed an application which resulted in a spontaneous cure.

Once al-Mutawakkil was informed that the Imam was preparing a revolt against him. Thereupon, he ordered a detachment of the army to launch a raid on the Imam's residence. When the soldiers entered his house, they found him sitting on a mat, reciting the Holy Qur'an.

Not only al-Mutawakkil, but his successors' opposition to the Imam was fierce. After the death of al-Mutawakkil, al-Mustansir, al-Musta'in and al-Mu'tazz carried on the same mission of harassment against the family of the Imam.

al-Mu'tazz, understanding the uncontrollable and intense devotion of the people towards the Imam, eventually contrived the Imam's assassination. He got him poisoned through an ambassador which resulted in the Imam's death within a few hours. The martyrdom occurred on 26th *Jumada 'th-thaniyah* 254 AH, and his funeral prayer was conducted by his son, Imam Hasan al-Askari. The Imam was only forty-two years old at the time of death. The period of his Imamate was thirty-five years. He was buried in Samarra', Iraq.

*   *   *

الامام الهادى عليه‌السلام قال للمتوكل ، الخليفة العبّاسي :

« لاَ تَطْلُبِ الصَّفَاءَ مِمَّنْ كَدَرْتَ عَلَيْهِ ، وَلاَ ٱلْوَفَاءَ مِمَّنْ غَدَرْتَ بِهِ ، وَلاَ ٱلنُّصْحَ مِمَّنْ

صَرَفْتَ سُوءَ ظَنّكَ إِلَيْهِ ، فَإِنَّمَا قَلْبُ غَيْرِكَ لَكَ كَقَلْبِكَ لَهُ .

al-Imam al-Hadi, peace be on him, said to al-Mutawakkil, the `Abbasid caliph:

*   Do not expect honesty and purity of intention from someone who has suffered from your malice; do not expect loyalty from one to whom you have been disloyal; do not expect goodwill from someone whom you regard with ill-will: his heart towards you is the same as your heart towards him.

THE THIRTEENTH INFALLIBLE

THE ELEVENTH IMAM

THE HOLY SHRINE OF IMAM HASAN AL-ASKARI (A.S.)
AT SAMARRA' (IRAQ).

AL-HASAN IBN ALI AL-ASKARI
(Peace be on him)

Name: **al-Hasan**
Title: al-Askari.
Agnomen: Abu Muhammad.
Father's name: `Ali al-Hadi (an-Naqi).
Mother's name: Hadithah (or Susan).
Birth: In Medina,on Friday, 8th *Rabi`u 'th-thani* 232 AH.
Death: Died at the age of 28, in Samarra', on Friday, 8th
Rabi`u 'l-awwal 260 AH; poisoned by al-Mu'tamid, the
Abbasid ruler; buried in Samarra' (Iraq).

THE HOLY Imam Hasan al-Askari spent twenty-two
years of his life under the patronage of his father, Imam
Ali al-Hadi (an-Naqi) after whose martyrdom he became
his divinely commissioned Imam.

Imam Hasan ibn Ali al-Askari, the son of the Tenth
Imam, was born in 232/845 and according to some Shiite
sources was poisoned and killed in 260/872 through
the instigation of the Abbasid caliph al-Mu'tamid. The
Eleventh Imam gained the Imamate, after the death of
his noble father, through Divine Command and through
the decree of the previous Imams. During the seven years

167

of his Imamate, due to untold restrictions placed upon him by the caliphate, he lived in hiding and dissimulation *(taqiyyah)*. He did not have any social contact with even the common people among the Shi`ite population. Only the elite of the Shi'ah were able to see him. Even so, he spent most of his time in prison.

There was extreme repression at that time because the Shi `ite population had reached a considerable level in both numbers and power. Everyone knew that the Shi'ah believed in the Imamate, and the identity of the Shiite Imams was also known. Therefore, the caliphate kept the Imams under its close supervision more than ever before. It tried through every possible means and through secret plans to remove and destroy them. Also, the caliphate had come to know that the elite among the Shi'ah believed that the Eleventh Imam, according to traditions cited by him as well as his forefathers, would have a son who was the promised Mahdi. The coming of the Mahdi had been foretold in authenticated *hadith* of the Prophet in both Sunni and Shi`ite sources.. For this reason the Eleventh Imam,. more than other Imams, was kept under close watch by the caliphate. The caliph of the time had decided definitely to put an end to the Imamate in Shi'ism through every possible means and to close the door to the Imamate once and for all.

Therefore, as soon as the news of the illness of the Eleventh Imam reached al-Mu'tamid, he sent a physician and a few of his trusted agents and judges to the house of the Imam to be with him and observe his condition and the situation within his house at all times. After the death of the Imam, they had the house investigated and all his female slaves examined by the midwife. For two years the secret agents of the caliph searched for the successor of the Imam until they lost all hope.

The Eleventh Imam was buried in his house in Samarra' next to his noble father.

Here it should be remembered that during their lifetime the Imams trained many hundreds of scholars of religion and *hadith,* and it is these scholars who have transmitted to us information about the Imams. In order not to prolong the matter, the list of their names and works and their biographies have not been included here.

قال الإمام العسكريّ عليه السّلام :

«إنَّ لِلْجُودِ مِقْدَارًا فَإذَا زَادَ عَلَيْهِ فَهُوَ سَرَفٌ ، وَلِلْحَزْم مِقْدَاراً فَإذَا زَادَ عَلَيْهِ فَهُوَ جُبْنٌ ، وَ لِلاِقْتِصَادِ مِقْدَاراً فَإذَا زَادَ عَلَيْهِ فَهُوَ بُخْلٌ ، وَ لِلشُّجَاعَةِ مِقْدَاراً فَإذَا زَادَ عَلَيْهِ فَهُوَ تَهَوُّرٌ. وَكَفَاكَ أَدَباً تَجَنُّبُ مَا تَكْرَهُ مِنْ غَيْرِكَ .

al-Imam al-Hasan al-`Askari, peace be on him, said:

* Generosity has a limit, which when crossed becomes extravagance; caution has a limit which when crossed becomes cowardice; thriftiness has a limit, which when crossed becomes miserliness; courage has a limit, which when crossed becomes fool-hardiness. Let this moral lesson suffice: refrain from doing anything which you would disapprove of if done by someone else.

THE FOURTEENTH INFALLIBLE

THE TWELFTH IMAM

THE SACRED CELLAR *(SARDAB)* AT SAMARRA' (IRAQ).

MUHAMMAD AL-MAHDI
(Peace be on him)

Name: **Muhammad**.
Title: al-Mahdi, al-Qa'im, al-Hujjah, al-Gha'ib, Sahibu'z-
Zaman, Sahibu 'l-Amr.
Agnomen: Abu 'l-Qasim.
Father's name: al-Hasan al-`Askari.
Mother's name: Narjis.
Birth: In Samarra', on Friday, 15th *Sha'ban* 255 AH.

He is still living and will appear before the end of the
world.
Minor Occultation: 8th *Rabi`u 'l-awwal* 260 AH.
Major Occultation: 10th *Shawwal* 329 AH.

THERE EXISTED a good deal of harmony and uniformity
between the aspects pertaining to the births of Prophet
Muhammad, the last Apostle of Allah and Imam al-Mahdi,
the last Apostolic Imam. Just as the coming of the Holy
Prophet was prophesied well in advance by the preceding
prophets, similarly the impending news of the gracious
birth of Imam al-Mahdi was foretold by the Holy Prophet.

173

Innumerable traditions in this context, quoted right from the Holy Prophet, from the glowing contents of many books of *Masanid, Sihah* and *Akhbar,* and of Shiite scholars (*ulama'*) existed. Many Sunni scholars have accumulated these traditions in complete volumes also, e.g.: *al-Bayan fi akhbar Sahibi 'z-Zaman* by al-Hafiz Muhammad ibn Yusuf ash-Shafi'i and *Dhikriyyatu 'l-Mahdi* by al-Hafiz Abu Nu'aym al-Isfahani as well as *as-Sahih* of Abu Dawud and *as-Sunan* of Ibn Majah. All of the above books record the traditions bearing evidence of the coming of this Holy Imam.

The promised Mahdi, who is usually mentioned by his title of *Imamu 'l-`Asr* (the Imam of the Period) and *Sahibu 'z-Zaman* (the Lord of the Age), is the son of the Eleventh Imam. His name is the same as that of the Holy Prophet. He was born in Samarra' in 255/869 and until 260/874 when his father was martyred, lived under his father's care and tutelage. He was hidden from public view and only a few of the elite among the Shi'ah were able to meet him.

After the martyrdom of his father he became Imam and by Divine Command went into occultation *(ghaybah)*. Thereafter, he appeared only to his deputies *(na'ib)* and even then only in exceptional circumstances.

The Imam chose as a special deputy for a time `Uthman ibn Said al-`Amri, one of the companions of his father and grandfather who was his confident and trusted friend. Through his deputy the Imam would answer the demands and questions of the Shi'ah. After `Uthman ibn Said, his son Muhammad ibn `Uthman al-`Amri was appointed the deputy of the Imam. After the death of Muhammad ibn `Uthman, Abu 'l-Qasim al-Husayn ibn Ruh an-Nawbakhti was the special deputy, and after his death Ali ibn Muhammad as-Samuri was chosen for this task.

A few days before the death of Ali ibn Muhammad as-Samuri in 329/939 an order was issued by the Imam stating that in six days `Ali ibn Muhammad as-Samuri would die. Henceforth the special deputation of the Imam would come to an end and the major occultation *(ghaybatu 'l-kubra)* would begin and would continue until the day God grants permission to the Imam to manifest himself.

The occultation of the Twelfth Imam is, therefore, divided into two parts: the first, the minor occultation *(ghaybatu 's-sughra)* which began in 260/872 and ended in 329/939, lasting about seventy years; the second, the major occultation which commenced in 329/939 and will continue as long as God wills it. In a *hadith* upon whose authenticity everyone agrees, the Holy Prophet has said, "If there were to remain in the life of the world but one day, God would prolong that day until He sends in it a man from my community and my household. His name will be the same as my name. He will fill the earth with equity and justice as it was filled with oppression and tyranny."

On the Appearance of the Mahdi:

In the discussion on prophecy and the Imamate it was indicated that as a result of the law of general guidance which governs all of creation, man is of necessity endowed with the power of receiving revelation through prophecy, which directs him toward the perfection of the human norm and the well-being of the human species. Obviously, if this perfection and happiness were not possible for man, whose life possesses a social aspect, the very fact that he is endowed with this power would be meaningless and futile. But there is no futility in creation.

In other words, ever since he has inhabited the earth, man has had the wish to lead a social life filled with happiness in its true sense and has striven toward this end. If such a wish were not to have an objective existence it would never have been imprinted upon man's inner nature, in the same way that if there were no food there would have been no hunger. Or, if there were to be no water there would be no thirst and if there were to be no reproduction there would have been no sexual attraction between the sexes.

Therefore, by reason of inner necessity and determination, the future will see a day when human society will be replete with justice and when all will live in peace and tranquillity, when human beings will be fully possessed of virtue and perfection. The establishment of such a condition will occur through human hands but with Divine succour. And the leader of such a society, who will be the saviour of man, is called in the language of the *hadith,* the Mahdi.

In the different religions that govern the world such as Hinduism, Buddhism, Judaism, Christianity, Zoroastrianism and Islam there are references to a person who will come as the saviour of mankind. These religions have usually given happy tidings of his coming, although there are   naturally certain differences in detail that can be discerned when these teachings are compared carefully. The *hadith* of the Holy Prophet upon which all Muslims agree, "The Mahdi is of my progeny," refers to this same truth.

There are numerous *hadiths* cited in Sunni and Shi`ite sources from the Holy Prophet and the Imams concerning the appearance of the Mahdi, such as that he is of the progeny of the Prophet and that his appearance will enable human society to reach true perfection and the full realization of spiritual life. In addition, there are numerous other traditions concerning the fact that the Mahdi is the son of the Eleventh Imam, Hasan al-Askari. They agree that after being born and undergoing a long occultation the Mahdi will appear again, filling with justice the world that has been corrupted by injustice and iniquity.

As an example, `Ali ibn Musa ar-Rida (the Eighth Imam) said, in the course of a *hadith,* "The Imam after me is my son, Muhammad, and after him his son `Ali, and after Ali his son, Hasan, and after Hasan his son *Hujjatu '1-Qa'im*, who is awaited during his occultation and obeyed during his manifestation. If there remain from the life of the world but a single day, Allah will extend that day until he becomes manifest, and fill the world with justice in the same way that it had been filled with iniquity. But when? As for news of the `hour;' verily my father told me, having heard it from his father who heard it from his father who heard it from his ancestors who heard it from `Ali, that it was asked of the Holy Prophet, `Oh Prophet of God, when will the "support" (al-Qa'im) who is from thy family appear?' He said, `His case is like that of the Hour (of the Resurrection). *He alone will manifest it at its proper time. It is heavy in the heavens and the earth. It cometh not to you save unawares*   (Qur'an, 7:187).' "

Saqr ibn Abi Dulaf said, "I heard from Abu Ja'far Muhammad ibn `Ali ar-Rida (the Ninth Imam) who said, 'The Imam after me is my son, Ali; his command is my command; his word is my word; to obey him is to obey me. The Imam after him is his son, Hasan. His command is the command of his father; his word is the word of his father; to obey him is to obey his father.' After these words the Imam remained silent.' I said to him, `Oh son of the Prophet, who will be the Imam after Hasan?' The Imam cried hard, then said, `Verily after Hasan his son is the awaited Imam who is "*al-Qa'im bi 'l-haqq*" (He who is supported by the Truth). "'

Musa ibn Ja'far Baghdadi said, "I heard from Imam Abu Muhammad al-Hasan ibn `Ali (the Eleventh Imam) who said, `I see that after me differences will appear among you concerning the Imam after me. Whoso accepts the Imams after the Prophet of God but denies my son is like the person who accepts all the prophets but denies the prophethood of Muhammad, the Prophet of God, upon whom be peace and blessing. And whoso denies (Muhammad) the Prophet of God is like one who has denied all the prophets of God, for to obey the last of us is like obeying the first and to deny the last of us is like denying the first. But beware! Verily, for my son there is an occultation during which all people will fall into doubt except those whom Allah protects."

The opponents of Shi'ism protest that according to the beliefs of this school the Hidden Imam should by now be nearly twelve centuries old, whereas, this is im possible for any human being. In answer it must be said that the protest is based only on the unlikelihood of such an occurrence, not its impossibility. Of course, such a long lifetime or a life of a longer period is unlikely. But those who study the *hadiths* of the Holy Prophet and the Imams will see that they refer to this life as one possessing miraculous qualities. Miracles are certainly not impossible nor can they be negated through scientific arguments. It can never be proved that the causes and agents that are functioning in the world are solely those that we see and know and that other causes which we do not know or whose effects and actions we have not seen nor understood do not exist. It is in this way possible that in one or several members of makind there can be operating certain causes and agents which bestow upon them a very long life of a thousand or several thousand years. Medicine has not even lost hope of discovering a way to achieve very long life spans. In any case, such protests from "Peoples of the Book" such as Jews, Christians and Muslims are most strange for they accept the miracles of the prophets of God according to their own sacred scriptures.

The opponents of Shi`ism also protest that, although Shi'ism considers the Imam necessary in order to expound the injunctions and verities of religion and to guide the people, the occultation of the Imam is the negation of this very purpose, for an Imam in occultation who cannot be reached by mankind cannot be in any way beneficial or effective. The opponents say that if God wills to bring forth an Imam to reform mankind, He is able to create him at the necessary moment and does not need to create him thousands of years earlier. In answer it must be said that such people have not really understood the meaning of the Imam, for in the discussion on the Imamate it became clear that the duty of the Imam is not only the formal explanation of the religious sciences and exoteric guidance of the people. In the same way that he has the duty of guiding men outwardly, the Imam also bears the function of waldyah and the esoteric guidance of men. It is he who directs man's spiritual life and orients the inner aspect of human action toward God. Clearly, his physical presence or absence has no effect in this matter. The Imam watches over men inwardly and is in communion with the soul and spirit of men even if he be hidden from their physical eyes. His existence is always necessary even if the time has not as yet arrived for his outward appearance and the universal reconstruction that he is to bring about.

قال الإمام الحجّة عليه السّلام :

« اعْلَمْ، إِنَّهُ لَيْسَ بَيْنَ اللهِ عَزَّوَجَلَّ وَبَيْنَ أَحَدٍ قَرَابَةٌ، مَنْ أَنْكَرَنِي فَلَيْسَ مِنِّي. وَأَمَّا
ظُهُورُ الْفَرَج فَإِنَّهُ إِلَى اللهِ، وَكَذِبَ الْوَقَّاتُونَ. فَأَمَّا وَجْهُ الأَنْتِفَاع بِي في غَيْبَتِي فَكَالأَنْتِفَاع
بِالشَّمْسِ إِذَا غَيَّبَتْهَا عَنِ الأَبْصَارِ السَّحَابُ، وَإِنِّي أَمَانٌ لأَهْلِ الأَرْضِ. وَأَكْثِرُوا مِنَ الدُّعَاءِ
بِتَعْجِيلِ الْفَرَج فَإِنَّ ذَلِكَ فَرَجُكُمْ.»

al-Imam al-Hujjah, peace be on him, said:

* Rest assured that no one has a special relationship with Allah. Whoever denies me is not my (follower). The appearance of the Relief (al-faraj) depends solely upon Allah; therefore, those who propose a certain time for it are liars. As to the benefit of my existence in Occultation, it is like the benefit of the sun behind clouds where the eyes do not see. Indeed, my existence is an amnesty for the people of the earth. Pray much to Allah to hasten the Relief, for therein also lies the release from your sufferings.

A CHRONOLOGICAL LIST OF THE FOURTEEN INFALLIBLES
THE HOLY PROPHET, HIS DAUGHTER AND THE TWELVE HOLY IMAMS

NOTE: Where there are differences of opinion on the dates of birth or death, the most popular view has been quoted.

Designation	Agnomen (Kunyah)	Name	Father's Name	Title (Laqab)	Date of Birth	Date of Death	Martyred by means of	Place of Burial
The Last Prophet of Allah	Abu'l-Qasim	Muhammad (Ahmad) (al-Mustafa)	'Abdullah	Rasulu'llah, Nabiyyu'llah, an-Nabiyy, Khatamu'n-Nabiyyin	17th Rabi' I, in the Year of the Elephant. (25. 8.570 AD)	28th Safar, 11 AH (25.5.632 AD)	Natural	Holy Medina al-Munawwarah, Saudi Arabia.
One of the Fourteen Infallibles	Umm Abiha	Fatimah	Muhammad	az-Zahra, as-Siddiqah, al-Batul, Sayyidatu'n-Nisa'.	20th Jumada II, in the fifth Year after the declaration of the Prophet-hood. (2. 1. 615 AD)	3rd Jumadi II, 11 AH (26. 8.632)	Injured	Holy Medina, Saudi Arabia.
1st Imam	Abu 'l-Hasan, Abu'l-Hasanayn, Abu Turab.	'Ali	Abu Talib	Amir al-Mu'minin, al-Wasiyy, al-Murtada, (Haydar).	13th Rajab, 10 Years before the declaration of the Prophethood. (25.5.600 AD)	Struck on 19th Ramadan (25th January); Died on 21st Ramadan 40AH(27.1.661AD)	Sword - while he was engaged in prayers.	Holy an-Najaf al-Ashraf, Iraq. (al-Ghariyy)
2nd Imam	Abu Muhammad	al-Hasan	'Ali	al-Mujtabi, as-Sibt (al-Akbar)	15th Ramadan, 3 AH (1. 3. 625 AD)	7th Safar, 50 AH (6. 3. 670 AD)	Poison	Holy Medina, Saudi Arabia.
3rd Imam	Abu 'Abdillah	al-Husayn	'Ali	Sayyidu'sh-Shuhada', as-Sibt (al-Asqhar)	3rd Sha'ban, 4 AH (8.1. 626 AH)	10th Muharram, 61 AH (10.10. 680 AD)	Sword -in the Battle of Ashura	Holy Karbala (at-Taff), Iraq.
4th Imam	Abu Muhammad	'Ali	al-Husayn	Zaynu 'l-'Abidin, Sayyidu 's-Sajidin, as-Sajjad.	5th Sha'ban, 38 AH (6.1. 659 AD)	25th Muharram, 94/95 AH (31.10.712 / 20.10.713 AD)	Poison	Holy Medina, Saudi Arabia.

7.	5th Imam	Abu Ja'far	Muhammad	'Ali	al-Baqir	3rd Safar, 57 AH (16.12.676 AD)	7th Dhi'l-hijjah, 114 AH (28.1.733 AD)	Poison	Holy Medina, Saudi Arabia.
8.	6th Imam	Abu 'Abdillah, Abu Musa.	Ja'far	Muhammad	as- Sadiq	17th Rabi' I, 83 AH (20. 4. 702 AD)	25th Shawwal, 148 AH (14. 12. 765 AD)	Poison	Holy Medina, Saudi Arabia.
9.	7th Imam	Abu 'l-Hasan (al-Awwal = The First), Abu Ibrahim	Musa	Ja'far	al-Kadum, al-'Abd as-Salih, al-'Alim.	7th Safar, 129 AH (28.10. 746 AD)	25th Rajab, 183 AH (1. 9. 799 AD)	Poison	Holy al-Kazir yyah, Iraq.
10.	8th Imam	Abu 'l-Hasan (ath-Thani= The Second)	'Ali	Musa	ar-Rida	11 th Dhi'l-qi'dah, 148 AH-(29.12.765AD)	17th Safar, 203 AH (24.8.818 AD)	Poison	Holy Mashhad (Tus-Khura Iran.
11.	9th Imam	Abu Ja'far (ath-Thani= The Second)	Muhammad	'Ali	at-Taqi, al-Jawad.	10th Rajab, 195 AH (8. 4. 811 AD)	30th Dhi 'l qi'dah, 220 AH (25. 11. 835 AD)	Poison	Holy al-Kazir yyah, Iraq.
12.	10th Imam	Abu 'l-Hasan (ath-Thalith= The Third) ,	'Ali	Muhammad	an-Naqi, al-Hadi.	2nd Rajab, 212 AH (27.9.827 AD)	3rd Rajab, 254 AH (28.6.868 AD)	Poison	Holy Samar (Surra-man-ra Iraq.
13.	11th Imam	Abu Muhammad	al-Hasan	'Ali	al-'Askari	8th Rabi' II, 232 AH (3.12. 846 AD)	8th Rabi' I, 260 AH (1.1. 874 AD)	Poison	Holy Samarra Iraq.
14.	12th Imam	Abu 'lqasim	Muhammad	al-Hasan	al-Mahdi, al-Qa'im, al-Hujja, al-Gha'ib, Sahebuz-Zaman Sahibu 'l-Amr, al-Muntazar.	15 th Sha'ban, 255 AH (29. 7. 869 AD)	Still alive, but in occultation.	- -	- - - -

www.ingramcontent.com/pod-product-compliance
Lightning Source LLC
Chambersburg PA
CBHW031513120626
46545CB00005B/1859